THE COLLAGE OF GOD

MARK OAKLEY

FOREWORD BY
WENDY COPE

DARTON · LONGMAN + TODD

First published in 2001 by
Darton, Longman and Todd Ltd
1 Spencer Court
140–142 Wandsworth High Street
London SW18 4JJ

Reprinted 2001

ISBN 0–232–52359–2

A catalogue record for this book is available from the British Library.

Designed by Sandie Boccacci
Phototypeset in 11¾/13pt Perpetua by Intype London Ltd
Printed and bound in Great Britain by
The Bath Press, Bath

Thanks are due to the following for permission to reproduce copyright
material: Bloodaxe Books Ltd for 'Raptor' by R. S. Thomas, taken
from *No Truce with the Furies* (1995); J. M. Dent for 'The Empty Church',
'Somewhere', 'Adjustments', 'The Kingdom', 'After Jericho',
'Kneeling' and 'Directions', all taken from *Collected Poems 1945–1990*;
Faber and Faber Ltd for 'The Way' by Edwin Muir, taken from *The
Complete Poems*, 'Lightenings' by Seamus Heaney, taken from *Seeing
Things*, 'Chorus III' by T. S. Eliot, taken from 'The Rock', 'Song VIII'
by W. H. Auden, taken from *Collected Poems*, 'Whitsunday in
Kirchstetten' by W. H. Auden, taken from *Collected Poems*; 'Strugnell's
Christian Song' and 'Some More Light Verse' by Wendy Cope, taken
from *Serious Concerns*; Oxford University Press for 'The Minister' by
Anne Stevenson, taken from *The Collected Poems 1955–1995*.

*For
Nanny and Bill
with love
and
gratitude*

. . . thus the human imagination, here as always, uses what it knows well in pursuit of efforts to move towards what it does not yet comprehend.

Margaret Donaldson, Human Minds: An Exploration

contents

foreword

Early in 1995 I was invited to do a poetry reading at the American School in St John's Wood. After the reading a young man who had been in the audience introduced himself as 'a local curate', and told me he sometimes used my poems in his sermons. Of all the things that have been said to me about my work, this was the most surprising. All my published work had been written at a time when I thought of myself as an atheist, and there were quite a few poems I wouldn't have chosen to show to a curate. Yet this one preached about them and not, it seemed, as examples of wickedness and folly.

After that we corresponded a bit, and I invited Mark to lunch – an occasion that turned out to be the beginning of a friendship I value. He is very good company, and I knew before I read it that this book would be good company too. Part of Mark's charm is his ability to laugh at himself, and I'm glad to see that it has found its way into the text. The picture of the newly-ordained Reverend Oakley behaving 'as if I were an extra from a *Miss Marple* film' made me laugh out loud. It occurs to me that a willingness to see the funny side of oneself is an essential quality in a clergyman, although I'm not sure how those who control entry to theological colleges could test for it.

That this book is sometimes amusing and always readable is no surprise, but I must confess to being even more impressed than I expected by the author's range of reference. Mark has been too busy telling funny stories to let me know just how well read he is. The pieces for this collage have been collected from many different centuries, many different places, many different kinds of writing – theology, philosophy, poetry, prose fiction, biography, theatre studies. Other pieces come from visits to the theatre and cinema. And some are the fruits of Mark's own experience – moving stories about people he has known, telling reflections of his life and work and on the Church and Christianity today. To have composed this wealth of material into such a concise and coherent book is a considerable achievement.

As it happened, three or four months before I first met Mark, I had begun going to church again after a gap of more than thirty years. Having moved from London to Winchester, I went to the cathedral to listen to the music. The music was – and is – wonderful, but it wasn't the only thing to draw me back again and again. I was deeply moved by the words of the Book of Common Prayer, remembered from childhood, and by the setting in which this marvellous act of worship was taking place. I became one of those people Mark refers to in Chapter Three, for whom 'beauty of stone, liturgy and music' lead to an 'interest in the possibilities of God'.

As I continue to explore those possibilities I shall be glad to have this book with me. I've read it twice – from now on I shall dip into it, knowing that on almost every page there is something I want to be reminded of, so that I can keep it in my own collage of God.

WENDY COPE
November 2000

THE COLLAGE
prologue

If a man learns theology before he learns how to be a human being, he will never become a human being.

Ludvig Holberg

We are made like quilts, over time and with many hands, drawn together into what we are and not knowing which stitch it is that makes us whole; which stitch, if removed, would unravel the entire fabric.

Erica Wagner

A PERSONAL TRIBUTE

In 1992, as part of my theological training for ordination, I worked in the chaplaincy team of St Mary's Hospital in Paddington, London, for five weeks. I was asked by my college tutor to keep a daily diary, monitoring each day's events and any theological reflections that might be prompted by them. I came to rely on that diary; for those weeks in June and July, at one of the busiest hospitals in this country, upturned my life. I had arrived, on my first day, very keen, a little hesitant perhaps but extremely confident in my belief in God. I was to leave, exactly one year before my ordination was due, angry, upset and equally confident that I would not be returning to college. For the rest of the summer I was restless. I stopped going to church. I began thinking about what else I could do with my life. Eventually, I painfully admitted that I had lost my faith.

I still have the diary I kept and am able to remind myself of the day-to-day experiences that I had at St Mary's. They are similar, of course, to those lived through by hospital chaplains and medical staff the world over. I remember one day in particular. The extract in the diary for it, 12 July 1992, reads:

> Today I was called on the bleep to one of the wards. As usual I spoke to the nurse first, in order to find out the facts of the situation and the prognosis of the patient. She told me of Chris, a 24-year-old man, who had just been admitted. He had been ill off and on for two years and had been in the same ward for periodic treatment during this time. He had no partner but was being looked after by his parents aged, I guess, in their mid-fifties.
>
> Chris was now very ill with Kaposi's sarcoma, lymphoma and dementia. I was told that the doctors had decided not to treat Chris. He was so acutely ill that there was little they could do. Their decision had only just been made and the parents were going to be told shortly. The parents had made it clear up till now, though, that treatment should always continue up until the very last minute. It was not going to be easy to help them accept the reality of the situation. The nurse had called for a chaplain to be around, knowing that the family was registered as being Anglican.
>
> When I entered Chris's room I saw how ill he was. The KS lesions disfigured his appearance and his dementia was evident. Sitting on either side of the bed were his

parents. As soon as I went in I sensed their anger. We talked together a little and I spoke to Chris, holding his hand and telling him who I was. I think he probably registered something of this. His parents left the room to see the doctors and I was left alone with Chris. We sat silently together, always holding hands and sometimes even hugging. We had only just met but we both knew that Chris had little time left to live. I tried to pray silently but was unable. I was angry too. Why had God allowed this suffering? Chris was only a year older than me and at most had a couple of days to live. Surely his parents had every right to be angry?

When Chris's parents returned I held them and listened as they cried and spoke of their frustration and their disappearing hopes for their son. 'I used to believe in God,' Chris's mother raged at me, 'I find it so difficult to now.' All I could say quietly to her was, 'So do I.' She looked at me and her anger towards me seemed to go. 'I'm pleased . . . so . . . pleased you've said that,' she replied. But why? All I had done was be honest. Was I really to be praised for that?

Chris died a few hours later when I had gone home. I never saw his parents again but I was constantly plagued by thoughts of their pain and anguish. What had been the point of Chris's life and had his parents' lives been scarred for ever? I felt that to hold hands and to listen was all I could offer (and I do see this as a positive contribution in a busy place such as a hospital), but I couldn't find the words to validate my ultimate reason for being there at Chris's bedside – to share the love of God? Yes; but where was it? All those theological words I have treasured seem despicable, and all those paperback books published on God and illness simply feel like attempts to sanctify the irredeemable. Lord, I think I believe. Help my unbelief.

I needed help quickly. Voltaire once commented that God made man in his own image and man returned the compliment. I could see now how I had crafted God just as I wanted him but he was not big enough to contain the experiences I had never had before. I was thrown into the realisation that my faith had been built rather like a Wendy house. It had nicely painted and, I had thought, secure walls which kept me in and others out and which enabled me to act out my psychological fantasies without much contact with those passing by. Now, though, the weather had changed and the winds of tragedy and fear had blown down my little proud construction and I didn't know where to take shelter. God had shattered in pieces around my feet and I felt alone.

I was very fortunate during those days, and in those that followed, to have some loyal and wise friends to support and see me through this time.[1] They helped me to relax, to believe that a world can be re-thought and that God might yet dwell in new and unexplored territory. This was not easily believed. In many ways it still isn't. However, after a few weeks and the difficult decision to return to college for the new term to discern whether I could or should carry on, I did start to 'pick up the pieces' and wonder if they could be placed together but, this time, with a different patterning. I somehow decided to attempt a refreshed commitment to the trek that faith demands rather than to the security of the Wendy-house walls that it is too often tempted to build around itself.

I am still gathering together those fragile fragments, thoughts, moments, words, hints and guesses from the past and present, six years later. This book is my tribute to those who were there, and still are, to help me hold them together somehow and who taught me to try and see again. In no way should these reflections be seen as some achievement or spiritual breakthrough. They are my way of trying to store something of the current colours and textures of my faith. Likewise, I hope that I do not criticise any particular beliefs or churchmanship. Rather I am critical of a complacency I find within myself and which I know, from talking with others of differing approaches and traditions, has been discovered by them along the way too. Such recognition is, unfortunately, not just discovered once in one's lifetime, but again and again. But I believe that each moment of such recognition can be turned into a step of salvation. I have often felt guilty during the last few years about admitting that I cannot find God where others tell me he is, and that there are days, and months, when I feel that there is no God to be enjoyed because the darkness, like that which descended at Chris's bedside, is too suffocating and random. At these times I need my friends again, both those I know personally and those I have befriended through their writing. I have learned that God is to be shared before he is ever understood.

THE COLLAGE OF GOD

Isaiah Berlin's careful and cautious essays have helped me to try and keep a sense of proportion when thinking through issues. In a famous essay on Tolstoy's view of history,[2] he noted that writers and philosophers (and perhaps human beings in general) can be divided into two distinct groups. On the one hand, there are those who see the world in terms of one organising principle, an overarching system in which they think, feel and understand. Using a line from fragments of the Greek poet Archilochus which may be translated as 'the fox knows many things but the hedgehog knows one big thing', Berlin concluded that such people are like the hedgehog, relating to a single central vision. Hedgehogs, he said, include such thinkers as Plato, Dante, Hegel and Nietzsche.

On the other hand, there are the foxes who

> pursue many ends, often unrelated and even contradictory, connected, if at all, only in some *de facto* way, for some psychological or physiological cause . . . These lead

lives, perform acts and entertain ideas that are centrifugal rather than centripetal; their thought is scattered or diffused, moving on many levels, seizing upon the essence of a vast variety of experiences and objects for what they are in themselves . . .[3]

Well-known foxes, he continued, include Aristotle, Erasmus, Molière and Joyce.

Berlin's thesis is that Tolstoy was a fox who wanted to be a hedgehog. The great Russian writer knew that there was such a thing as 'truth', a framework and foundation for everything that exists. He was conscious, though, that he had never seen it face to face and as he grew older he became more and more conscious, not of a single belief system to interpret by, the 'one', but 'always, with an ever-growing minuteness, in all its teeming individuality, with an obsessive, inescapable, incorruptible, all-penetrating lucidity which maddens him, the many.'[4] We live today in the time of the 'many'. Never before have we seen so much, had so much communicated to us, had so many choices laid before us. It is difficult to keep up with the fast and furious way the globe revolves. Where can we turn for help to interpret, not only the events of the world, but our own lives? Although there are other ways, a literate people will most often turn to words. As the narrator, Ruby, concludes in Kate Atkinson's recent novel *Behind the Scenes at the Museum*: 'In the end, it is my belief, words are the only things that can construct a world that makes sense.'[5]

Like Tolstoy, although many today seek a comprehensive and compact package of truth in which to place their trust and by which to live their lives, they are at the same time only too conscious of the riot of interpretations of the world on offer. We have become aware of the cultural, psychological and political shaping of 'truth' through the years. We have never had so many words thrown at us on screens and pages, but at the same time we have never so distrusted them, conscious as we are that in a competitive and litigious time words will boast, trick and try to sell. The individual only need self-consciously reflect for a short while on the change in perceptions and understanding that has occurred in his or her own life to see how fragile and fluid our beliefs can be. To try and 'make sense' of the world will always entail some sort of imaginative construction and it will certainly mean being conscious of the language we employ to do this, seeking those words that are still able to reverberate within our inner spaces.

This book is written for theological foxes who, grateful as they may be for the insights and profundity contained within systematic Christian doctrine, ultimately remain unconvinced that reality is mirrored neatly in the recitation of any creed. It is for those who have become increasingly aware in their Christian discipleship that faith is more of a synthesis than a system and that nothing is 'simply one thing'.[6] Faith can only live and breathe in the Holy Spirit, the Spirit who is both Comforter and Disturber. Faith is not a proud self-consistent philosophy. It involves maintaining oneself between contradictions that can't be solved by analysis. It is therefore a living response to the grace of God as revealed in fragile lives. It resembles a collage. Collages are slowly pieced together out of diverse materials in an attempt to present a portrait whose integrity is found in its variety and creativity. A collage of Christian faith will be built out of the Christian traditions and texts, the myriad experiences of human living, imagination, silence and prayer. This is not to deny the concept of revelation. On the contrary, I want to argue here that 'truth' for those who journey with God is not to be defined by the rational criteria of verification and falsification. It can instead be understood as meaning 'manifestation', letting what shows itself be, by the creative grace of God. No one has ever seen God, says St John. He is made known.

Unlike a tome of systematic theology, this book has no beginning, middle and end. It attempts to be unapologetically poetic in its resisting of any such closure. W.H. Auden once said that the work of a poem is never finished, just abandoned. It is the same with theological reflection. This is a collection of thoughts on the life of faith as I have experienced it over a short number of years and, en route, it thanks our poets and novelists for illuminating the world, in which this life of faith walks, by their own particular and fresh naming of it. Such literary art has proved to be for me, using Robert Frost's expression, 'a momentary stay against confusion'. The first reflections here examine those theme-materials I have found myself using most in my collage-making; the second pay homage to those who have helped me piece them together. Such a collage is likely to be smiled at by some because it is not as neat, or as clever, or as beautiful as their own cherished pictures. I understand this only too well. In the end, though, all of us who journey the Christian way are unable to prove any of our beliefs except, perhaps, by the way in which we translate them into the lives we live.

Finally, then, there has to be a humility in the theological fox. Humility has been described by Iris Murdoch as a 'selfless respect for reality'.[7] Such respect is our vocation and, as such, is to be found in the judicious Cardinal of one of Isak Dinesen's *Last Tales* who, when asked by a penitent whether he was absolutely sure that it was God he served, answered: 'That, Madame, is a risk which the artists and the priests of the world have to run.'[8]

part one
MATERIALS

one
HIDDENNESS

Vere, tu es Deus Absconditus . . .

Isaiah 45:xv

. . . any religion which does not say that God is hidden is not true.

Blaise Pascal

Humility pierceth the clouds . . .

Ecclesiasticus 35:xvii

Due to a couple of biographies being published at the time of my writing, there is an increasing public interest in the life and work of Dennis Potter. Potter was an acclaimed television dramatist whose works include such popular plays as *Pennies from Heaven* (1978) and *The Singing Detective* (1986). On St Valentine's Day 1994, Potter was diagnosed as having cancer of the pancreas with secondary cancers in the liver. He was told that, realistically, he had only a small number of weeks left to live. He was fifty-eight years old. As time passed he naturally grew weaker and needed more liquid morphine to help see him through the day. He disciplined himself, however, to get up each morning and work on a script he was determined to finish. A few weeks before he died, Melvyn Bragg asked him if he would give an interview. He said yes, as long as it was early in the morning when he had his strength, and if he could call it a day and end the interview when the pain became too much to bear.

On 5 April this interview took place on Channel Four television. It is a fascinating and often disturbing revelation of a man whose words are carefully distilled by his approaching death. Bragg begins by asking Potter about the discovery of his cancer. He then asks about God. Has he thrown him off? Potter replies:

> Religion as always been − I've said it before, it doesn't matter that I repeat myself, I won't get many more chances to repeat myself, thank God − but religion has always been the wound, not the bandage. I don't see the point of not acknowledging the pain and the misery and the grief of the world, and if you say, 'Ah but God understands' or 'Through that you come to a greater appreciation . . .' I mean, I don't think, well you nasty old sod, if that's God . . . that's not God, that's not my God, that's not how I see God. I see God in us or with us, if I see at all, as some shreds and particles and rumours, some knowledge that we have, some feeling why we sing and dance and act, why we paint, why we love, why we make art. All the things that separate us from the purely animal in us are palpably there, and you can call them what you like, and you can theologise about them and you can build great structures of belief about them. The fact is they are there and I have no means of knowing whether that thereness in some sense doesn't cling to what I call me.[1]

Potter was an irritant all his life to the Establishment and the conventional, challenging any agnosticism as much as any orthodoxy. Here, in this late reflection, I think he pinpoints something essentially important for those with faith to remember, namely that belief in God comes out of an intuition, a sense of awe, surprise, beyondness, epiphany. It emerges from the perception that reality can somehow, ultimately, be trusted.

'That's not how I see God . . . if I see at all.' Potter voices a complaint, though, against some thinking about God whose concepts cannot be faithfully internalised with integrity in the light of his contemporary experience and understanding. He is not alone in wanting to find a new language for expressing the wonder of being alive and attributing life to a divine source and, at the same time, to be honest in admitting the inevitably human and limited boundaries of our knowledge. The poet Richard Wilbur reveals this condition:

> All that we do
> Is touched with ocean, yet we remain
> On the shore of what we know.[2]

Potter is also aware that there are times when he does not 'see' God. As I have said in the Prologue, such times can be disturbing and they can feel destructive. During my short ordained ministry I have often tried to speak about this shadowing of God and have been silenced by the related stories people tell in return. It has become evident to me that on the whole we do not find it easy to talk about faith's darkness and yet we discover both companionship and release when we do. The difficulty in speaking lies in our notions of betrayal and failure. Not only do we think that we must be doing something wrong to feel as we do (when others appear so strong and content) but we also feel we are betraying God by our talk of his seeming absence.

It is essential to the journey that we find a way through these fears. They are damaging to our wholeness and they are not companions of the Judeo-Christian tradition in, and from which, our faith lives and breathes. Many will know how awkward and frustrating it can be, as we enter our own adulthood, to befriend a parent. For some of us, our struggle for identity, our confusions in the ordering of what our past is doing now, will not always allow us to settle into an immediate and comfortable relationship with a father or mother. For many such a friendship will come much later on in life. For some people, of course, it never establishes itself at all. There is surely an analogy to be made here with our relationship with God. The journey begun at baptism is one into a divine mystery, a dance of twists and turns, and on this journey every ready, cheap and seductive answer has the nature of imprisonment and death:

> Friend I have lost the way
> *The way leads on*
> Is there another way?
> *The way is one.*
> I must retrace the track
> *It's lost and gone*
> Back I must travel back
> *None goes there none.*
> Then I'll make here my place
> *(the road leads on)*
> Stand still and set my face.
> *(the road leaps on)*
> Stay here forever stay
> *None stays here none.*
> I cannot find the way.
> *The way leads on.*
> Oh places I have passed
> *That journey's done*
> And what will come at last?
> *The road leads on.*[3]

We are being encouraged more and more today to be consumers. It should not surprise us if such a society is impatient,
demanding a return for payment and tempted to treat Christian
faith within a similar framework, expecting quick spiritual
'highs' in return for some exchange with God. Such a consumerist approach to faith fails to understand the pilgrimage
nature of Christian discipleship, in which we are called to be
citizens, not consumers, of the Kingdom of God. Consumers
end up having a lot to live with but little sense of what to live
for. Citizens grow in self-awareness and attend to the needs of
those they share the privilege of life with, for the sake of the
common good. They do not demand everything so that they
can somehow enjoy life, but instead they ask for life in all its
fullness that they might enjoy all things with profound gratitude to the One who is life's source.

Similarly, in a world of information and fact-production that
has extended rationality to all areas and all levels of reality, we
are tempted to reduce everything from the Mysterious to the
Problematic and are suspicious of languages that speak of what
is not seen. 'If you describe the world just as it is,' said
Tolstoy, 'there will be in your words nothing but many lies and
no truth.' Similarly, Gerard Manley Hopkins reminded his
friend Robert Bridges that whereas Bridges meant just an
'interesting uncertainty' when he used the word 'mystery',
Hopkins meant 'an incomprehensible certainty'.[4] Hopkins
knew that a world obsessed with itself will only ever be
puzzled by a commitment to a travelling faith that celebrates
both the visible and invisible. Mary Bryden, in a recent essay on
research into the life of St Thérèse of Lisieux makes an illuminating observation: 'contemporary interest tends to focus
much more on the psychology of sainthood than on its super-
natural manifestations: clues as to what fires an individual to
remain consistently committed to a perceived ideal excite
more curiosity than the pursuit of signs and miracles'.[5]

So, we find ourselves divided in two. There are those who

are not content until they 'solve' the problem and categorise everything, like some nineteenth-century botanical clergyman, and there are those who are contemplative, 'embracing the mystery', and who refrain from trying to manage the world and all the surprises it contains. A.S. Byatt writes of an associated division:

> you must learn now, that the important lesson – as long as you have your health – is that the divide is not between the servants and the served, between the leisured and the workers, but between those who are interested in the world and its multiplicity of forms and forces, and those who merely subsist, worrying or yawning.[6]

This division is found in our churches too.

I shall now risk making a sweeping generalisation. On the whole, religious people fall into two basic categories. First, there are those who want to *resolve* the mystery of God, to teach and preach it clearly, to spell out the facts as they are believed, to be like a reporting journalist ('our God correspondent') and relay information in black and white language to those not in 'the know'. On the other hand, there are those who, instead of wanting to resolve the mystery, seek to *deepen* it. Such people are uneasy with such words as 'simply' or 'easily', they are willing to get tongue-tied, to say 'I don't know', to embrace the evocative multi-layered languages of poetry and music in their search for God. They have come to believe that truth is not the same thing as the elimination of ambiguity.

I suppose that people today generally view the Church as more of a group of resolvers than deepeners. Certainly those in the media professions prefer a resolver. The Church is expected to have a message, to know what it stands for, and to be able to check its delivery of production too. How this latter exercise is achieved is debatable, but it is usually phrased in terms of 'success' (financial, doctrinal, moral, social etc.) and thought to make itself known by the large number of people attending church services.

The Church, of course, does have a gospel to proclaim and embody. To deny this would be to dig up its very roots and see it wither away in a cold and indifferent climate. Faith in this gospel is the theme of this book. But, and here I lay my cards on the table as a preferred deepener rather than resolver, part of that belief in the gospel involves a humility on the part of those who hold it in their hearts. For Christians throughout the ages have acknowledged that God is both *omninominabile* and, at the same time, *innominabile*. That is, all true words speak of the Holy One who is, but no word or name can ever contain, capture, control or reveal him in his fullness – least of all, we learn in prayer's stillness, one uttered by me.

This is where most of us are caught as we try and express our belief and our love – between the power of word and image, of our genuine human need for narration and the discovery that is born in our language and, on the other hand, the knowledge that as soon as our words are spoken they die and linger on to be misunderstood. We learn that there is an education to be found in silence. One saint of the Church once mused that bishops reflect God most when they keep quiet . . .

This place of tension is theology's home. Any theology which travels far from this territory fails to be 'theo'-logy. In Ian McEwan's recent novel *Enduring Love* a man and his girl-friend witness an event that changes their life. Later on, they sit in a kitchen and talk about their day: 'we were back in our seats, leaning over the table like dedicated craftsmen at work, grinding the jagged edge of memories, hammering the unspeakable into forms of words, threading single perceptions into narrative . . .'[7] This could be a good working description of ecclesial theology. The Church calls on her memory as stored in the Scriptures, ancient texts and traditions. Memory inspires, as the ancient Greeks knew. Without a memory we are immobile and anonymous, and our resources for the future become limited and lifeless. Memory revitalises, encouraging us to shape our own telling, our language and poetry, and not to be afraid to add our own stories and perceptions to the whole. We remember for our future. Sometimes there will be a clash between what our forbears perceived and what we believe, but theology is, as yet, unended and the mysterious dance that continues often involves radical steps of change. The irony is that by taking such steps we so often see the footprints of those who have gone before us come more clearly into view, but in a different light.

Part of me worries that the contemporary Church is losing aspects of its wide and generous memory and therefore condemning itself to become a 'swimming pool Church' – one that has all the noise coming from the shallow end. In such a paddling pool it will be easy to say 'easy' and mysterious to say 'mysterious'. It will also be a place where the Dennis Potters, and all those who say that they are having difficulty seeing, will not feel welcome or at home. This will be a Church more interested in self-indulgence, imposed boundaries and small interest groups. It will be fearful of truthful and genuine debate and will lack the confidence to form friendships. Such a Church will never be able to help teach souls to fly.

Certainly a critical part of our faith's memory that is being overlooked in some quarters today is the tradition that speaks so eloquently of the *hiddenness* of God and of the discovery of human equality, one with another, in our quest to 'live, and pray, and sing, and tell old tales, and laugh . . . and take upon us the mystery of things, as if we were God's spies'.[8] It is known that human beings will always be threatened by their irrational fears and will make enemies in order to project these fears onto others. Theology should be the antidote to this destructive activity. Theology is one of God's invitations to listen to one another. It is also God's opportunity of letting us know, in often tantalising ways, that he always lies just beyond our reach, forever ancient and forever new.

In our conversations with faith's memory, and with its contemporary experiences, we learn that God often seems to hide himself from our view. Those who recoil at this thought, believing that it is not somehow in keeping with the God who reveals his loving ways at each and every turn of history's passing, often misunderstand what is being said here. For it would appear that our forbears learned that God does not hide himself to be indifferent or hardened towards us. Strangely, he hides himself in order to make himself more known. In the words of one philosopher: 'when we come to accept a revelation of the hidden God, what is revealed is revealed as hidden'.[9]

There is in the heartland of our faith's life and understanding what has been called a 'fiery dance' between piety and a sense of dereliction. The God whom we seek to worship is also the God who vanishes from sight and who leaves us longing for him, even despairing that he might never return to us. I am writing these thoughts a few days after having celebrated Ascension Day with its Gospel reading: ' . . . and lifting up his hands he blessed them. Now as he blessed them, he withdrew from them . . .'[10] The God of blessing is the God who is often removed by clouds.

As we know from St Luke's second volume, the Acts of the Apostles, God reveals himself in the vitality of Holy Spirit, a freshness that demands new languages for the God we too often think we understand. This Spirit is described as both 'Comforter' and 'Disturber'. It is the same God who instils peace and energy who also instils from time to time a sense of loss and the consequent renewed desire to seek his face, even in the deepest shadows. Graceful irritants are placed in the soul in order to nurture its growth.

In the Gospel of St John, Jesus tells the Pharisees that it is because they say that they can see that their guilt remains.[11] It is the blind man in the story who draws out Jesus' compassion and interest. It is the one who cannot see who is led through a healing process in which he is taught to see afresh. Those who can't see their own need for such renewal will only ever see the failures of others contrasting with their own righteousness. They will be unable to perceive the work of God when it conflicts with their tidy expectations. But it is exactly from such expectations, too often small and comfortable, that God hides himself. God's hiddenness encourages us to 'unlearn', to crack prejudice and break the shells we form around ourselves. Clement of Alexandria observed: 'Most people are enclosed in their mortal bodies like a snail in its shell, curled up in their obsessions after the manner of hedgehogs. They form their notion of God's blessedness by taking themselves for a model'.[12] To fight the spiritual paralysis that sets in when God is so trapped in our nets is to acknowledge that 'there is an age when one teaches what one knows. But there follows another when one teaches what one does not know. It comes, maybe now, the age of another experience: that of unlearning . . .'[13] In the life of spiritual pilgrimage, then, there comes a time when we 're-cognise', give renewed attention, and slowly begin to 'recognise' him who is beyond in our midst.

To study our faith tradition as to how God has taught souls to spread their wings, instead of just preen them from time to time, is to frequently encounter his hiddenness. Moses 'drew near to the thick darkness where God was' to be instructed for the future that 'in every place where I cause my name to be remembered I will come to you and bless you';[14] Jacob wrestles with the unknown in order to receive blessing;[15] Job continues to seek God in the midst of loss and affliction; and the Psalms frequently voice a sense of abandonment and complaint.[16]

St Gregory of Nyssa, in his *Life of Moses*, illustrates the theological understanding of God's hiding:

> What now is the meaning of Moses' entry into the dark-
> ness and of the vision of God that he enjoyed in it? . . .

The sacred text is here teaching us that . . . as the soul makes progress, and by a greater and more perfect concentration comes to appreciate what the knowledge of truth is, the more it approaches the vision, and so much more does it see that the divine nature is invisible. It thus leaves all the surface appearances, not only those that can be grasped by the senses, but also those which the mind itself seems to see, and it keeps on going deeper until by the operation of the Spirit it penetrates the invisible and incomprehensible, and it is there that it sees God. The true vision and the true knowledge of what we seek consists precisely in not seeing, in an awareness that our goal transcends all knowledge and is everywhere cut off from us by the darkness of incomprehensibility.[17]

Christian reflection on the knowledge of God born in not seeing has been done by some of the Christian faith's best-loved thinkers and prayers, from John of the Cross to Charles Wesley. I was introduced to many of them when I first studied theology at university but my over zealous rationality liked perfect solutions. I remember being rather rude to my Doctrine professor when I told him that his motto seemed to be 'For all your doctrinal headaches take Paradox'. Now I am beginning to understand differently and to appreciate that God's truth often nestles in ambiguity, darkness and painful contradiction. How else could it be when, at the very heart of the redemption story, where God is revealed most perfectly, Christ cries out at the God who appears to have forsaken him? 'The Trinity is present to all things,' reminded Denys the Areopagite, 'though not all things are present to it.'

The hidden God inspires our longing. We will stop desiring him if we think we ever possess him. In the eternal life that we are called to by Christ we celebrate the physical and spiritual truth that eyes are to be both opened and closed, that we have eyelids, that we need times of rest, renewal, dreams and tears. To see all, understand all, would be damaging for any soul on earth for it would singe it with completeness and finality. We must always beware, reminds Rubem Alves, of the seduction of clarity and the deceit of the obvious.[18] God calls us beyond them.

The greatly missed priest and poet, R.S. Thomas, whose work has sustained me through many shadowed days, wrote a poem entitled 'The Empty Church' in which he puzzles over his thoughts that God is unlikely to be attracted by any 'spiritual' bait we put down:

> They laid this stone trap
> for him, enticing him with candles,
> as though he would come like some huge moth
> out of the darkness to beat there.
> Ah, he had burned himself
> before in the human flame
> and escaped, leaving the reason
> torn. He will not come any more
> to our lure. Why, then, do I kneel still
> striking my prayers on a stone
> heart? Is it in hope one
> of them will ignite yet and throw
> on its illumined walls the shadow
> of someone greater than I can understand?[19]

Thomas's work very often confronts the hidden God and testifies to the fact that if faith is threatened today by anything it is by various forms of impatience. In 1976, he delivered a lecture at the National Eisteddfod at Cardigan. He called the lecture 'Abercuawg' and began by asking:

> Where is Abercuawg? I'm not certain that this is the right
> way of asking the question. I'm half afraid that the answer

to that is that it does not exist at all. And as a Welshman I do not see any meaning in my life if there is no such place as Abercuawg, a town or village where the cuckoos sing.[20]

Thomas searches for the place but on each arrival finds that this is not Abercuawg. He denies the hope that one day he will find it, though, for it is by the emerging sense of something lost that the true sense of Abercuawg takes a seize upon us. He uses this analogy for the God-search:

This is man's condition. He is always about to comprehend God; but inasmuch as he's a creature and finite, he will never succeed. Nor will he ever see Abercuawg. But by trying to see it, by longing for it, by refusing to accept it belongs to the past and has gone to oblivion, by refusing to accept something second hand in its place, he will succeed in maintaining its eternal possibility.[21]

This 'eternal possibility' is the One who calls us into being and who cradles us. He is also the one who is unseen and often unfelt but the quest for him persists:

Surely there exists somewhere,
as the justification for our looking for it,
the one light that can cast such shadows?[22]

No matter, then, how some Christian brothers and sisters might make us feel uncertain in our talk of God's hiddenness and of the darkness where we say, retrospectively, that God was. 'There is in God (some say) a deep but dazzling darkness'[23] and there is in the heart of God a divine call to his people to keep journeying, to keep longing for freshness and discovery. The more one approaches God the hungrier one becomes for him. Relating to God, as in all our loving relationships, can only be done in the context of both nearness and distance. In the distance that sometimes opens up lie possibilities. These possibilities change lives:

> For nothing can be sole, or whole
> That has not been rent.[24]

An anonymous man once wrote a prayer which, I feel sure, came out of his faith in the God who hides himself and so makes himself known. In the words of this prayer we can see how God dissolves stale expectation and forges the one gift that was made to live in the courageous heart – thankfulness:

> I asked for strength that I might achieve;
> I was made weak that I might learn humbly
>   to obey.
> I asked for health that I might do greater things;
> I was given infirmity that I might do better things.
> I asked for riches that I might be happy;
> I was given poverty that I might be wise.
> I asked for power that I might have the praise
>   of men;
> I was given weakness that I might feel my need
>   of God.
> I asked for all things that I might enjoy life;
> I was given life that I might enjoy all things.
> I received nothing that I had asked for;
> but everything that I had hoped for.
> Almost despite myself my unspoken prayers
>   were answered;
> I am, amongst all men, most richly blessed.[25]

It is the hiddenness of God which reveals our poverty in and of ourselves. We learn that hiddenness is actually grace seen from another angle, it is the foundation of God's transforming work. David Jones, in his preface to *The Anathemata*,[26] reflects that his intention is not to edify nor persuade but rather to uncover. For this is what a mystery does, he continues. At root the word 'mystery' implies a closing, but mysteries are meant to disclose too, to show forth, and by so doing, 'to set up'. The mystery of God's hiddenness, though often interpreted as such, is not closure and self-concealment but a persistent revealing of God's self for the nurture of those he loves. Ultimately it is the shadowing of God that draws us to the light, inspiriting our ache to be within his Kingdom.

In her recent novel *Fugitive Pieces*, Anne Michaels records a conversation between a young man, Jacob, and his elder friend Athos whilst out walking. It is a conversation worth remembering by those of us who are often confused by our life with God:

> "We were discussing religion."
>
> "But Athos, whether one believes or not has nothing to do with being a Jew. Let me put it this way: The truth doesn't care what we think of it."
>
> We ascended the valley. The hills were scorched with sumac and sedge, cloudy with fraying thistles and milkweed. I could see patches of sweat darkening Athos's shirt.
>
> "Maybe we should rest."
>
> "We're nearly at the top. Jacob, when Nikos died I asked my father if he believed in God. He said: How do we know there's a God? Because He keeps disappearing."[27]

two
DISCOVERY

*Meanwhile, man, precisely as the one so threatened,
exalts himself and postures as lord of the earth. In
this way the illusion comes to prevail that
everything man encounters exists only insofar as it
is his construct. This illusion gives rise in turn to
one final illusion: it seems as though man
everywhere and always encounters only himself.*

Martin Heidegger

*I greet Him the days I meet Him, and bless
when I understand.*

Gerard Manley Hopkins

*Patches of God — light in the woods of
our experience.*

C.S. Lewis

In her novel *A Map of the World*, Jane Hamilton sees a divide
between how two people may understand God. She writes:

'For Theresa, God was something that was outside her, some unfathomable being who made the highway radiant. I thought in the harsh December wind that for me God was something within that allowed me, occasionally, to see.'[1]

If God is hidden, but can be referred to and celebrated within our languages, it is also understood by the tradition of faith that he can be discovered and experienced in epiphanies and unveilings. The two thoughts of God mentioned by Hamilton are both owned by Christian people, for although God is unfathomable and Other, God is also imprinted within us, moving amongst us and, as we see in the ministry of Jesus, continually opening eyes and ears to life as it is nurtured and willed by him. This entails that we should be constantly on the alert, like wedding guests looking in the distance for the arrival of the bride, and that, as Philip Toynbee says, 'the basic command of religion is not "do this!" or "do not do that!" but simply "look!"'[2]

John Searle, in his interesting work *Mind, Language and Society*, makes an observation about humankind:

> It is characteristic of our conscious experiences that they typically refer beyond themselves. We never just have an isolated experience, but it always spins out to further experiences beyond. Each thought we have reminds us of other thoughts. Each sight we see carries reference to things unseen. I call this feature overflow . . .[3]

For those who believe that a God sustains and breathes his life into this universe, there is to be an overflow of a similar nature as they make endless connections and seek him out daily. In his sermon at St Paul's Cathedral on Christmas Day in 1624, the Dean, John Donne, taught the congregation that God 'comes to thee, not as in the dawning of the day, not as in the bud of spring, but as the sun at noon to illustrate all shadowes in harvest, to fill all penuries, all occasions invite his mercies, and all times are his seasons'.[4]

But what does it mean to glimpse God, to discover something of God's glory? Many people, including violent murderers, tell us that they have seen God and that he has told them to do this or that. How can we distinguish in ourselves a valid testimony? For Christians, the answer lies in the internal dialogue of the Christian community. We are able to test our experiences by relating them to those that our tradition has been privileged to know through its ages. For many of us, experiences of God are grasped retrospectively or, in the words of T.S. Eliot, 'we had the experience but missed the meaning'.[5] It does not surprise me that the God who hides himself should reveal himself indirectly in this way. How else would we be able to bear such revelation? Although some Christians will tell you that God spoke to them on a particular day and time, I can only relate my own experience of his revelation, namely:

> We never catch
> him at work, but can only say,
> coming suddenly upon an amendment,
> that here he has been.[6]

This is not to say, however, that I do not have moments of great peace and a sense of God's presence with me – usually in times of prayer and reflection. We need to be cautious, though, in speaking of the truths we think we have learned through such important times. Our learning is slow and clumsy, our understanding is always trying to catch up with our intuitions. We know more than we are able to say. Such moments of peace are for our encouragement and comfort. They are rarely the sharing of a sacred manifesto for immediate delivery. Jesus' own teaching ministry was very much grounded in his need to pray alone before he talked with his friends, and then indirectly by story and parable. It is not that

God reveals everything in Christ and through his Spirit. It is that he reveals all we need to know and love.

The Christian tradition teaches that God is discovered in a variety of reflective ways. He is encountered, for instance, in engagement with the Scriptures. This library of texts, ranging from poems to letters and ancient stories to hymns, is described as being holy because of the encounter with the eternal God that men and women have had through a responsible reading of its pages. There are those who are convinced that to be holy it has to resemble the factual pages we can easily access on the Internet, inerrant information about God. But as any engaged student of the Bible will tell you, the texts are not always consistent and are gloriously varied in their outlook. How else could it be? The Bible is the best example of a collage of God that we have. It contains different views, experiences, beliefs and prayers and yet, although not systematic in its portrait of God, it is where Christians glimpse something of the divine being and his life in the world. It is where they have found a vocabulary for the Christian life. The texts of the Bible are from disparate eras, cultures and authors but, held together, they form a colourful and intriguing picture that draws us into its own landscape.

The Bible, as a place of encounter and shared experience, should never be put on a pedestal. It has no need of one. Rather, it is to be befriended as the companion to faith it is. Friends are loved, debated with, sometimes disagreed with, and are the ones we enjoy spending time with because of what we learn about ourselves, and them, in this dialogue of trustful exchange.

Similarly, as we befriend the Scriptures throughout our journey we will discover and understand something of God and human existence. Sometimes the understanding will be created out of tension and dispute, in Socratic fashion. Sometimes it will be because a part of the Scriptures resonates deep within our inner spaces. In all this loving and lively friendship between the voices of our inheritance and the voices of today, we know that we engage in a hallowed affair of the heart and mind.

Interpretations of words and phrases will differ among us. Our theologies will disagree as a result of reading the same pages. It is simply the case that thoughts divide us. Where we must unite is in our agreement of the pages being a place of sacred encounter and of others' interpretations being a contribution to the shared Christian inheritance, just as our own are. Argument and debate, of course, might also be a divine dwelling place because they warn us against monomania – a special temptation to the religious personality. We have talked so much as if unity means uniformity. These words refer to different things. As celebrants of diversity (interpretative, cultural, social, racial, sexual, political) and for a proper sense of proportion as a Church before God, as individuals alongside each other, our uniformity as a Christian body has never been and will never be. It is unity for which we pray and it will only ever be revealed as authentic if there are shades of difference amongst us.

John Dominic Crossan has described his own work as the attempt to find out 'what a future theology might look like once the literary imagination has been unleashed on the Bible'.[7] He particularly likes to study the disorienting and undermining parables which, he argues, 'give God room' by shattering 'the deep structure of our accepted world', eroding our built-up defences and opening us up to the transcendent. It is not only the parables but the Scriptures themselves that hold this possibility within and it is the whole host of different readers, with their varied readings, celebrating this fact that works towards a unity, born in a God who is discovered within time.

Another place in which God has been encountered is that of human relationship. If we spy God in friendship with the Scriptures, we also find him in the gift of human love. God's energy can be embraced in a relationship with a partner, friends, family or those for whom we dislocate our selfish centre. We allow them to find a place at our centre too. The birth of a child, the death of someone special, the expressions of love and shared affection, the joy of eating together, talking, laughing and crying with someone who has begun to under-stand us – all these and the many other human encounters reveal that we live on fragile and holy ground in which some-thing of the wounded grace of God is visible. Elie Wiesel, in his intensely moving account of his imprisonment in concentration camps during the Second World War, asks a simple question: 'What is a friend? The person who first makes you aware of your own solitude and his, and helps you escape it so that you, in turn, may help him. It is thanks to him that you can fall silent without shame, and unburden yourself without loss of face.'[8] These words might have been written as an introduction to confession in a liturgy, so close are they to describing the merciful presence of God. They disclose the unveiling of this presence when a person loves another simply for being who he or she is. Those who love, says St John, know God in the deepest depths of their being. The commands to love God and to love your neighbour are caught up with one another and cannot be separated for both require a turning outwards of the heart. Such movement is a divine displacement and, as such, clears the way for secret and flickering communions with God.

Another source of holy discovery within the Christian com-munity has been that of remembrance. As the ancient Greeks knew, inspiration is the daughter of memory and it should not surprise us that Christians primarily claim an act of remem-brance as the place of encounter with their Lord. The eucharist is the place in which bread is broken and wine poured in remembrance of him who captures our deepest longings and affections. Just as the risen Christ in the Gospels appears to the disciples where he was first with them – seashores, upper rooms, gardens – so he does today in the simplicity of a shared meal, hidden within the elements of creation, and in the actions of thanksgiving, blessing and giving to those who open their hands in their desire to receive him.

When I was at theological college I had a friend whose mother was ill with Alzheimer's disease. Every time he went to visit her in the care home in which she resided her memory had deteriorated. Eventually she no longer remembered her son and their times together were painful to him as their usual ordinary, and wonderful, way of being together as mother and son had come to an end.

One day I saw my friend after he had visited his mum and found him very happy. Apparently this latest visit had been different. He had gone into her room as usual and sat down with his mother. Once again, she did not know him but she spoke to him politely. Then the nurse came into the room with some tea for them both. She set the tray down between them and, straight away, my friend's mum took charge. She picked up the teaspoon and stirred the pot of tea. She poured the milk into the cups and then poured the tea. She put two spoons of sugar in her cup and one into her son's. For this briefest of moments, a time of unspoken action, my friend saw the mother he had thought was lost. He had seen the same mum take charge over the teacups as she had always done in their home when they had been together there. This time of re-cognition had renewed my friend's belief that, although things were different now, the woman he visited was still his mum and would be forever.

His mum died only two weeks later but my friend never forgot the shared life that had been celebrated in a few seconds in a nursing home room. It seems to me that this story is eucharistic. For it is in the characteristic actions of Christ, taking, thanking, blessing and sharing, that we glimpse him amongst us again. We can feel as if we have lost him, or he us, and that the tragedy of our time clouds any recognition or communion. But as those first disciples were placed in the presence of the faithful and undefeated risen Christ and, as such, needed to admit their need of his forgiveness and patience, so we approach him. Our communion with him, splintered and fractured as it is, is always his communion with us for it is dependent upon his fidelity and not ours. Any theological or ecclesiological arguments that lose sight of this essential defining truth will always be in danger of becoming self-approving or of promoting communion with Christ as if it were similar to joining a gentlemen's club: 'If it is I who say where God will be, I will always find there a false God who in some way corresponds to me, is agreeable to me, fits in with my nature. But if it is God who says where He will be . . . that place is the cross of Christ'.[9] We slowly learn that we do not control the grace of God as it is shown to us in Jesus Christ.

It is, indeed, in the person of Jesus Christ that we discover God in human form. So vital is this unveiling of the Holy One that we name ourselves 'Christian' because our God is known most intimately through an encounter with Christ. There are those who teach that words, biblical texts or ancient liturgies channel the will of God in its most undiluted form. The Christian tradition, however, has taught through every generation that God is met in Christ and that, after this, every other discovery is a blessing. Our faith has found an enormous variety of images to describe this belief – the Word made flesh, Christ as God's only Son, the visible image of the invisible God.

Some images are more helpful than others in the passing of time. For me, Christ is the body-language of God, a living and breathing language of bodily and eternal love. In her poem 'Getting It Across', U.A. Fanthorpe gives a voice to Christ who is frustrated at his dense and slow disciples. He reflects on what he is doing amongst them and concludes:

I am tattooing God on their makeshift lives.[10]

The imprinting of God onto ordinary people has been discovered in Christian discipleship time and time again. It

appears that his life, teachings, death and celebrated resurrection have taught many people that there is another world and
that it can be lived within this one. This world has been given a
voice in Jesus Christ and these rumours of another way of
being intrigue, unsettle and compel us, as R.S. Thomas
unearths in his poem on 'The Kingdom':

> It's a long way off but inside it
> There are quite different things going on:
> Festivals at which the poor man
> Is king and the consumptive is
> Healed; mirrors in which the blind look
> At themselves and love looks at them
> Back; and industry is for mending
> The bent bones and the minds fractured
> By life. It's a long way off, but to get
> There takes no time and admission
> Is free, if you will purge yourself
> Of desire, and present yourself with
> Your need only and the simple offering
> Of your faith, green as a leaf.[11]

It is in the nature of love to want to express itself. God seeks to
disclose himself even though he never allows the whole truth
to be known. It is in the historical figure of Jesus, and the
Christ of faith, that God has thrown out his arms to hold us
close to himself. As A.M. Ramsey wrote: 'God is Christlike,
and in him there is no un-Christlikeness at all'.[12] It was the
frightened figures of humanity that nailed Jesus to the cross
and, as they did so, they found themselves caught up in an
intimate revelation of God.

When I was a student I disliked going to church on Good
Friday. My trained rational faculties kept disturbing my focus
in the liturgy. What was going on when Jesus was on the cross?
What did it all mean? What was God up to? I ventured one day

to tell one of my tutors about these thoughts and he confessed that the Good Friday service was his favourite precisely because such questions could not be answered and therefore, though not forgotten, could be laid aside for a while. 'The point perhaps,' he said to me, 'is that there is no meaning and we don't know what is going on. We just know that, in all this terror and pain, God is.' Christ on the cross displays a God taken out of all the wrappings we dress him in and puzzlingly unveils him and his suffering love against all our better judgement and understanding. This is God's body-language, non-verbal, expressive and communicating at levels not ordinarily channelled. It is said that the majority of human communication is done without language. It is the same, I believe, with sacred revelation.

When I was a hospice chaplain I started to see the value of such silence in the face of unexplainable and painful truths. We do not know why there is evil, pain and death. We will never know. All we can do is to have the courage not to cheapen or dilute them by fanciful logical thinking. Only those who suffer can, in retrospect, begin to formulate a framework for what it is they bear. The rest should remain in silence – or perhaps in complaint. For Jesus himself cried at the God who seemed to have forsaken him at the time when he had never been nearer to him:

> So man cried, but with God's voice.
> And God bled, but with man's blood[13]

Those who focus their prayers on the crucified Christ will never expect God to intervene, for it is in the nature of love not only to be expressive but to be limited by its vulnerability. They will only expect his presence. It was Etty Hillesum who prayed to God during the horrific events of the Holocaust: 'You cannot help us, but we must help You and defend Your dwelling place inside us to the last'. Can we say more than her?

I have found John V. Taylor's parable using Act IV of Shakespeare's *Henry V* enlightening. Before the battle of Agincourt, Taylor reminds us, the king moves incognito amongst his men and hears a honest man saying that the king will have a lot to answer for on the day of judgement when it is brought to light how much devastation and bloodshed he has allowed by his reckless adventure and design. Henry, though, knows what he is asking of these men and the burden laid upon them: 'we must bear all'. Taylor continues:

> yet he still believes it will prove worthwhile and, as morning breaks, he rallies his small force to believe in it with him, just as he will share the risks and the wounds with them. So he instils into them his own hope, his faith in the value of the enterprise.[14]

It is something of this type, concludes Taylor, that was being said by the Creator through the dying Jesus. A world of accident, freedom and pain is the only one able to respond freely and fully to his love. God still believes that the eventual outcome will outweigh the immense waste. Taylor ends:

> So, knowing we cannot understand, cannot forgive, what he is doing, God has come among us as a fellow human-being and fellow-sufferer to make amends and win back trust. Through his own abandonment and death that Given Self of our Creator calls us to share his hope as he shares our pain, to believe in his staggering, costly venture even while there is little evidence of it ever succeeding.
>
> > We few, we happy few, we band of brothers;
> > For he today who sheds his blood with me
> > Shall be my brother.[15]

It has been the conviction of Christ's followers that such suffering and death is not the end of the human story but that Christ was raised to new life, another disclosure of the nature of God's love. Love may be vulnerable and open to wounds but it is always fresh and capable of unleashing renewal. The great Easter sermon of John Chrysostom shakes us out of despair:

> Enter then into the joy of your Master . . .
> Let all enjoy the banquet of faith . . .
> Let no one weep for his sins: forgiveness is risen from the tomb.
> Let no one fear death: the Saviour's death has set us free . . .
> Christ is risen and life has prevailed![16]

Hope in the risen Christ gives freedom to the spirit to fight against what is deathly and covers up life in its fullness and potential. Resurrection faith incorporates us into a 'dancing day'. We are invited to experience the fresh awareness, openness and confidence of anyone taught the new steps of a dance, enticing so much out of us by including us within its pattern. There is much that disfigures our humanity but Christian hope proclaims this defeated by the transfiguring brought about by faith in Christ, the human image of the eternal God. Such transfiguration begins in this life of ours as we experience it now, resurrection can be spied through the darkest cracks of an imprisoned life: the tomb is split open when we make our way to Christ: 'Here ends the known. But, from a source beyond it, something fills my being with its possibilities.'[17]

Only in this hope can we begin to assemble together. In our fellowship, as sharers in this resurrection life, we can also discover God amongst us, in our neighbour and companions. Although I have a soap-dish doctrine of the Church where what is cleansing and vital is from time to time being held by something pretty mucky and unpleasant to handle, I believe that we urgently need a community of faith for it is a simple truth that human beings need each other. They need them to celebrate with, cry with, to correct and to encourage each other. By recognising our fears in the confident light of Christ we start a process in which we are able to prevent ourselves from falling into the trap of projecting them on to others and making them 'enemies'. This breaking down of our constructed walls of fear enables a different way of being together. It begins a new vocabulary where we greet our 'brothers and sisters in Christ', join in 'communion' and share 'peace'.

A search for God made alone is an isolated business and can be one full of selfish preoccupation. We should not dismiss the gift of company on our pilgrimage lightly for going it alone was not the way of Jesus, as he toured the countryside with his friends, nor was it the way promoted by the early Christians. It would be understandable if in a busy and stressful life people today sought God away from noise and pressure of human relating but the church is called to be a 'school of relating', offering a pattern of relationships and priorities that challenges those we find ourselves trapped in day to day. Dag Hammarskjold could see that image is quick to replace substance in individuals as well as institutions: 'A blown egg floats well, and sails well on every puff of wind – light enough for such performances since it has become nothing but shell, with neither embryo nor nourishment for its growth'.[18]

Release from shallow and unfulfilled relationships will not be found by isolation. It will come through the deepening of our relationships, raised awareness of each other, trust and the search for the common good. This will entail curbing the destructive cynicism we are developing about the possibility and potential of genuine relationships that build us up rather than force upon us our disintegration. The community that shares peace in the name of the risen and faithful Lord is the community that should have something to reveal to a world that wants a lot but expects little. It is a world tempted to replace commitment with consumerism. The narrator of one of Peter Hoeg's novels reflects whilst looking at a cake in a restaurant:

The raspberry tart has a bottom layer of almond custard. It tastes of fruit, burnt almonds, and heavy cream. Combined with the surroundings, it is for me the quintessence of the middle and upper classes in Western civilisation. The union of exquisitely sophisticated achievements and a nervous senselessly extravagant consumption.[19]

Shop windows make good mirrors and our reflected souls are too often lifeless and despairing. The Church should be a sanctified rebellion against such an empty vision of human life and love: 'We are in great haste to send and receive messages from outer space. But so hectic and often so tedious are our days, that many of us have nothing of importance to communicate to those close to us.'[20] The Christian message is clear: it is the reflection of God in Jesus Christ that offers back a life in all its overwhelming fullness. By attaching our freedom to Christ we begin to discover the image of God within us: 'The hearts of human beings were made great enough to contain God himself'.[21]

To be alert for the sake of revelation is part of our Christian vocation. The easy habit of becoming blind to what surrounds us, noted by Anna Akhmatova when she wrote that 'absence is the best medicine for forgetting . . . but the best way to forget forever is to see daily',[22] is to be fought against because to succumb entails living in a dull and colourless existence. We strive to develop what Merleau-Ponty called '*la foi perceptive*', a faith that perceives beyond and in the everyday – the intrinsic quality of the ordinary capable of striking through the sense and into the mind with a feeling of newness and discovery which Gerard Manley Hopkins tried to capture in his poetry. Those who search for the God who manifests himself and tempts us to find him for a moment before passing by will be like those described as the 'happy few' by Stendhal:

The happy few . . . are those who remain emotionally alive, who never compromise, who never succumb to cynicism or the routine of the second-hand. The happy few are not necessarily happy. But they are never corrupted and seldom bored. The happy few possess what Baudelaire calls 'impeccable naiveté', the ability to see the world always afresh, either in its tragedy or its hope.[23]

three
POETRY

The poet is the priest of the invisible.

Wallace Stevens

What we long for most eludes us.

James Cowan

*The power of poetry is that by simply naming
it can illuminate.*

Elizabeth Jennings

I have always enjoyed hearing the well-intentioned things that
children have written in essays and exams at school which, to
the teacher at least, have proved amusing. It is especially in
Religious Studies that words can get a little mixed up. One girl
once wrote about her favourite story in the Bible and informed
the reader that 'Noah's wife was called Joan of Ark'. Another
girl thought that 'the patron saint of travellers is St Francis of
the seasick' and one of her friends got words a little confused in
his ethics essay when he proudly declaimed: 'Christians can
only have one wife. This is called monotony.' My favourite,
however, is when the small boy wrote in his history exam that

'Henry VIII liked Wolsey so much that he made him a cardigan.' History might have been rather different if he had . . .

Although we can smile at the mistakes children make in their language, and therefore in their perceptions of reality, adults make similarly confident claims for their own words and wisdom. As I write this now myself, I believe we can all get it badly wrong and, perhaps, God smiles. It seems to me that those who seek to journey with God need to be conscious of their words and of the penitence needed as each one is spoken. Dag Hammarskjold noted in his famous *Markings*:

> Respect for the word is the first commandment in the discipline by which a man can be educated to maturity – intellectual, emotional and moral. Respect for the word – to employ it with scrupulous care and an incorruptible heartfelt love of truth – is essential if there is to be any growth in society or in the human race. To misuse the word is to show contempt for man. It undermines the bridges and poisons the wells.[1]

Many people feel that the language of faith is the purest of all, by which they usually mean that it is the most literalistic. What is spoken simply places a name to what is, language describes by referring to a 'fact'. This is a common approach today, perhaps extended because of the language of the Internet and the information culture. The devices by which meaning is achieved by language, of course, are much more complex than mere reference. We use metaphor, analogy, symbol and myth regularly to express the new and essential. Although we all utilise such ways of speaking and understanding day to day, there still persists a belief that language in its truest form, particularly religious language, is 'factual', mirroring reality by a description that should aim to be as simple as possible.

The literary critic Northrop Frye[2] has argued that such a confidence in the purpose of language arises out of generations of empiricism where 'common sense' dictates that truth is the same thing as a descriptive verbal structure. Any other truth-claims are deemed, at best, second rate. Such a view of language and truth impoverishes us all. Our basis for evaluating the truth is fragile and needs all the support it can get and such reductionism does not permit us to move beyond a literal meaning towards a new order of reality. George Orwell has taught us through his writings that in totalitarian states where dreams are crimes life is made monochrome with no mysteries or invisibility.

Similarly, to *describe* God as if he were laid out on a pathologist's table is an impossible task. We cannot see, feel and describe him as we can an object. Instead, we *relate* to God and our relational language consequently takes on the nature of the languages of love, awe and tears: 'Only after one has come to understand the way in which conventional wisdom seeks, and ultimately fails, to explain the world, can one begin to perceive it.'[3]

As soon as we encounter God we know that we are beginning a relationship in which our thoughts, feelings, words and grammar have to plead for a little forgiveness. We become aware of our idolatrous ability to drag God down to our own level with all its cultural and individual limitations. Even our proudest doctrinal statements, ones we may be willing to die for, need to humble themselves as they are professed. These doctrines are not written in a crude literalistic mode either. They are fighting for truth in a variety of figurative literary forms in the hope that something of the divine nature might be caught inside them. We know that the 'is or is not' character of some theological chatter leaves us untouched. In a now famous essay Matthew Arnold argued: 'Our religion has materialised itself in the fact, in the supposed fact; it has attached its emotion to the fact, and now the fact is failing it . . . the strongest part of our religion today is its unconscious poetry'.[4] There is no need for theology to be embarrassed about this state of affairs. In fact, in her languages (verbal, ritualistic and musical) lie theology's greatest gift to a generation suffering the 'curse of literalism'. If the Church gained more confidence in the figurative languages on which it is built it would feel more able to befriend the artists, writers and poets of today with more open and trustful willingness. Like birds hovering on the strong currents of the air we breathe, people of art and people of faith are keen to discern something of these currents which pull and shape our lives. It is an exciting task and one that might create many friendships and maybe even some agreement. It does not surprise me, then, that it is our cathedrals that, by their beauty of stone, liturgy and music, are housing some of the most reflective and lively partnerships between contemporary arts and faith. It is also our cathedrals, for the same reasons, that are attracting many people's interest in the possibilities of God. Human beings need intimation as well as specification.

In the church I serve in Covent Garden, I have been almost shocked by the number of young people who visit the church day by day to pray or draw on the building's quiet and sense of presence. Virtually every time I walk into church I find people, instead of looking around at the various memorials to actors, giving attention to what might be called 'the spiritual life'. Talking to many of them later, I have discovered that whereas the Church has been very keen to foster a sense of the nearness, immanence and intimacy of God over the last few years, it is the sense of transcendence that is causing them to pause. Much of these people's lives has been levelled down. The average worker or visitor to Covent Garden between the ages of eighteen and thirty wears the same clothes as her or his contemporaries, shops at the same boutiques (in whichever city or town in Europe), watches the same films, and eats the same food. It is only money that might pull a person out of this existence by offering alternative possessions and entertainments.

In all this stressful and yet rather humdrum living, there are those who turn their thoughts towards what has priority and urgency. The sense of the eternal, what matters and what might last of us, is still strong in a number of so-called 'secular' hearts. To find a vocabulary for this interest is awkward, though, as they have not necessarily inherited one equipped for the task, and the verbose, and often bland, liturgies of many Churches that treat imagination as if it were a vestigial organ, does not appeal to this compelling search for meaning, for the sacred. At its best, Christian language will capture something of both human longing and the divine meeting of it. In her poem 'The Minister', Anne Stevenson reflects at a time of a death as to why in today's world we may still have a role for an ordained person:

> We're going to need the minister
> to help this heavy body into the ground.
>
> But he won't dig the hole;
> others who are stronger and weaker will have
>   to do that.
> And he won't wipe his nose and his eyes;
> others who are weaker and stronger will have
>   to do that.
> And he won't bake cakes or take care of the
>   kids —
> women's work. Anyway,
> what would they do at a time like this
> if they didn't do that?
>
> No, we'll get the minister to come
> and take care of the words.
>
> He doesn't have to make them up,
> he doesn't have to say them well,

he doesn't have to like them
so long as they agree to obey him.
We have to have the minister
so the words will know where to go.

Imagine them circling and circling
the confusing cemetery.
Imagine them roving the earth
without anywhere to rest.[5]

It is as if a priest should be a poet-in-residence, capturing something of what it is to be human and pushing it up to heaven in the hope that nothing will be lost as God embraces it and indicates, as a lover might in teasing and gentle ways, that the words have been received within his being. He might even reply in a secretive, heart-rending expression of himself. All this will entail being a Church that, in William Blake's words, sees not with the eye but through it:

Unless the eye catch fire
    The God will not be seen.
Unless the ear catch fire
    The God will not be heard.
Unless the tongue catch fire
    The God will not be named.
Unless the heart catch fire
    The God will not be loved.
Unless the mind catch fire
    The God will not be known.[6]

Christian faith lives from the imagination and whereas there are some who find this threatening because they think it means faith will be fantastical, there are those who know that God's revelation of himself is too expansive and penetrating to be propositional. Revelation is addressed to the human imagination. The deepest truths are received in a person's whole being not just in his or her rational faculty. As one theologian, Paul Avis, has recently written: 'Christianity is a faith that subsists in the symbolic realm and is appropriated through imaginative indwelling'.[7] He concludes that the language of faith is able to refer but not describe and that its penetration of reality is heuristic not definitive. In other words, the theological art cannot be equated with philosophical analysis, scientific verification or mere biblical quotation. It was the philosopher Wittgenstein who confirmed that to be religious is to know that the facts of the world are not the end of the matter. Because God is both knowable and unknowable the tension of the symbol, the multilayers of the myth and the openness of the poetic are all vital to our desire to celebrate the Mystery to whom we relate and in whom we have our being. It may be because of this that the Psalms remain some of the most loved texts within the community of faith.

It is true that some theists have stressed the use of language, myth and symbol so much that God has been reinterpreted to the point of being almost lost. In the British theological world the most famous of these is Don Cupitt and the so-called 'non-realists'.[8] Each of these thinkers has a different approach, and Cupitt is always difficult to pin down for long (a characteristic that makes me enjoy his work), but in general terms the thesis is that if the word 'God' is spoken of in cosmic or objective terms it will just be a fossilised anachronism employed by escapist minorities.

Committed to the use of religious language, the non-realists nevertheless believe that there is only one reality and that is the realm of material things and living organisms. There is no personal God 'out there' giving ultimate meaning to the world. There are, for them, no absolutes. God exists *in mente* not *in re*, or, in Gertrude Stein's expression: 'there is no there there'. The Sea of Faith network, which provides a forum for such views and those who wish to explore them further, puts forward the following definition of non-realism: ' . . . the view that there is nothing beyond or outside human beings, neither God or some notion like Ultimate Reality which gives life meaning and purpose. We do that for ourselves'.[9]

How does this differ, then, from classical atheism? The non-realists feel committed to using religious language as an important instrument in expressing value and celebrating personal and communal ideals. Worship, likewise, it is believed, offers us ritualistic ways of connecting with ourselves and others, enabling us to craft the interests of a community in a unique way. Like Prospero, the non-realists concur:

> Now my charms are all o'erthrown
> And what strength I have's my own.[10]

Many people in our churches today would want to agree with the non-realists in saying that some of the agenda-crafted definitions of God in the past have not been healthy, wholesome or helpful. They certainly cannot be maintained today with integrity. However, as we have seen, we can acknowledge our limitations without having to erase realities. For many of us, to keep the language of faith whilst dismissing the concept of God to whom we can objectively relate is to keep the bath water whilst throwing out the baby. There is no doubt, though, that the non-realists are speaking in a voice that strikes a chord with part of the contemporary crisis of belief. Those people who visit our cathedrals, to whom I referred, may have sympathies with Cupitt and his friends because the beauty of the liturgy and architecture somehow speaks louder than the perceived narrow interpretation of life being presented in the life of the Church outside it.

So whilst agreeing that the non-realists have things to say that are beneficially corrective in some respects, I have to disagree with them in their finality (and certainty) regarding the non-objectivity of God. To discover our complexity and fallibility does not necessarily entail the vacancy of God. Relativism does not imply non-realism.

Those of us who are happier calling ourselves figurative or critical realists, do not wish to systematise our impatience with much that has been handed down to us so quickly and thoroughly. Scepticism about metaphysics is not the next step in revision of concepts of God that do not relate to our understanding and experience. I believe that through imaginative use of our faculties and their artistic creativity, and in dialogue with our magnificent spiritual inheritance, we may be able to 'apprehend in extremely partial and highly imagistic ways truths about reality beyond those that we apprehend through the other varied ways in which we learn from the world around us'.[11]

I have experienced, and continue to do so, a depth to life which is gift-like and which needs our attention. To believe in an objective holy God, rather than some sort of all powerful Celestial Controller, is no more incredible than believing that nothing exists outside of language. Conditioned art forms, literary or artistic, may well have an extra-human reference. Brian Russell compared our situation to that of someone on a foggy night looking at Lincoln cathedral.[12] The spotlights shine onto the beyondness of the cathedral which reaches back down into our midst; but the light is reflected towards us by the fog. There is only reflected light, but an impressive though inexactly identified reality beyond and within the light. I cannot believe that this is just a metaphysical fancy. It simply does justice to my intuition that there are more things in heaven and earth than are dreamt of in non-realist thought or, in the words of Rowan Williams, 'part of our difference is . . . that Cupitt actually cuts the Gordian knot of the objectivity of God, where I wish to go tracing on its several strands and trying to see why it has taken these particular contours'.[13]

To be boldly assertive about our imaginative and varied utilisation of words, then, is not to deny God's objectivity.

Indeed, it is exactly the opposite. I would not spend so much of my time and energy immersing myself in the patterns and stories of faith if I did not believe that within them I can be awakened to the divine and ultimate reality I call God.

For all the reasons I have cited so far, I believe strongly that the Church today needs to be a poetic Church. A poetic Church will be one that confidently uses its human imagination for the sake of sacred discovery, new angles from which to see the glory of God, and it will call on all its members to use their given gifts to these ends. Its theology should be inventive, fed by memory and deep-running, and as it delivers itself it should be both startling and oddly familiar – like all successful poetry. A poem by Seamus Heaney which tells the story of a vision experienced by monks in Clonmacnoise during the Middle Ages is enlightening:

> The annals say: when the monks of Clonmacnoise
> Were all at prayers inside the oratory
> A ship appeared above them in the air.
>
> The anchor dragged itself along behind so deep
> It hooked itself into the altar rails
> And then, as the big hull rocked to a standstill,
>
> A crewman shinned and grappled down the rope
> And struggled to release it. But in vain.
> 'This man can't bear our life here and will drown,'
>
> The abbot said, 'unless we help him.' So
> They did, the freed ship sailed, and the man climbed back
> Out of the marvellous as he had known it.[14]

In talking about this poem, Heaney said that it was 'about the way consciousness can be alive to two different and contradictory dimensions of reality' and still finds 'a way of negotiating between them'.[15] The image of the monks in awe at the vision but helping the ship on its way instead of laying hold of it and making a relic or fossil of it, is one that opens up an understanding of how we, as a Church, might view our approach towards the revelation of God which is, as George Herbert knew, 'heaven in ordinarie'.[16] Like trying to intercept a butterfly to see its markings and luminous wings, extending a hand only to find it has gone, so is theology responsive to God's revelation. Unfortunately, some confuse the butterfly pinned on velvet for it instead. It may be gorgeous, even reassuring somehow, but it is dead. An approach to God like this will start to define him but not experience him. Poetry, on the other hand, cannot be defined but only experienced. This reflects the Christian belief in God's manifestation in the world, in a human life and the Holy Spirit. The words with which the Church has expressed this belief continually need to be enlivened and made fresh in every generation.

Poetry, says Heaney, 'has to be a model of inclusive consciousness. It should not simplify. Its projections and inventions should be a match for the complex reality which surrounds it and out of which it is generated'.[17] This would do well as a working brief for the Church's theological enterprise. 'With Christians,' argued Cardinal Newman, 'a poetical view of things is a duty'.[18]

In my Christian discipleship I have found poetry indispensable. To begin with it has captured, briefly but uniquely, moments of recognition and epiphany, like 'matches struck in the dark'.[19] New journeys begin with such moments. I have also relied on what Heaney terms 'the redress of poetry', its ability to counterweight, balance and tilt the scales of reality 'towards some transcendent equilibrium'. This gives birth to transformed, if unexpected, understandings and an unveiling of denied potential. Poetry is as much of a process as it is representation. We can be grateful that poetry is and that it can help. Poetry has, by some, been called the language of paradox, polyvalence and ambiguity and I have treasured those poems that have committed themselves to holding together the contradictions of life and the world rather than give way to any simplified portrait of them. It is possible to be meaningful and imprecise. At its best, the Church has also done these things for me in its teachings, stories and liturgies. At its worst, when its poetic confidence has given way to the demands of the literal minded, it has shadowed, even deadened, my soul by its interpretation of them. It is the difference between life in all its fullness and existence in all its mediocrity.

> There is an aggression of fact
> to be resisted successfully
> only in verse, that fights language
> with its own tools. Smile, poet,
>
> among the ruins of a vocabulary
> you blew your trumpet against.
> It was a conscript army: your words,
> every one of them, are volunteers.[20]

The first language of faith, and its most vital, is that of worship. It is as we fall on our knees and bow down before the holiness, mercy, grace and pity of God that we struggle to find our voice: 'Human language is like a cracked kettle on which we beat out tunes for bears to dance to, when all the time we are longing to move the stars to pity'.[21]

Flaubert's sentiment is similar to that of the liturgist and a survey of the many different activities that can take place in liturgy's language reveals the exhausting task he or she has: 'assertions and statements, expressions of attitudes, thanksgiving, praise, blessing, confession, acclamation, pledge, exhortation, command, affirmation, testimony, agreement, evaluation, warning, dedicating, pardoning, declaring, greeting and praying'.[22] The liturgist knows the variety and juxtaposition of linguistic functions, the different speech categories (e.g. unison, dialogue and monologue) and the changes in mood, pace and rhythm, that all co-exist in the work of communal worship. The French language distinguishes between *langage* and *langue,* where *langage* is the holding together of diverse ways of communicating in a unified purpose. It is clear to even the most casual participant in a liturgy that liturgical language is not a precise, scientific or necessarily sharp theological language. Liturgy is not a purely verbal act. It is more akin to a theatrical performance. Liturgy is able to dramatise what is often lost in the abstractions of systematised thought and speech, namely the human implications of particular doctrines. A language for liturgy needs to be sensitive to the greater purposes of liturgy as a whole and adopt itself accordingly. As one commentator has put it: 'Liturgical texts may not be theological treatises belonging to the specialized language-games of pure science or, in other words, worship has its own style and must be on guard against the intrusion of ideologies and the habit of theologising'.[23] The liturgist has an artistic vocation and needs to be assured that multivalence and ambiguity do not reduce the authority of his or her language. Liturgy will be demeaned by an obsession with the prosaic and will quickly become inauthentic when made didactic. It will be inspirited, on the other hand, by a poetic assurance that there is not just one meaning to discover in the sacramental quest through life. It is more a matter:

> Of heart's truth, mind's inheritance,
> From one to another told and retold.[24]

When we read Gail Ramshaw's account of the Easter liturgy we can see how the Church has grounded itself on a ritualised poetics:

An example of the poetry that is liturgical language is the

Exultet . . . Here in the middle of the dark night a single burning candle is lauded as the greatest light the world has seen. Rather than talk about Christ and the resurrection, the chant sings of the light and the night. The light is the "splendour of the eternal King", and it shines brightly throughout the world enrobing the church in its fire. The candle is an icon before us, becoming other than it is, receiving us other than we are, as the chant transforms words into other than they appear . . . In perhaps the most dizzy collage of images, the morning star arises from the grave to find one single candle burning, vanquishing night and itself becoming a beacon of light. Where our recently purchased paschal candle stops and where Christ takes over, it is impossible to say.[25]

A poetic Church will be at home when engaged in such worship. When words are cheapened by over use or impoverished by systematic precision, the gift of the word becomes a curse of chatter:

I have given you speech, for endless palaver,
I have given you my Law, and you set up commissions.[26]

A Church responsive to its poetic vocation will be watchful of its words and their patterning and crafting. Jargon threatens language; slogans beat down principles; strong ideas can be substituted by thin novelty. In her Nobel speech in 1996 the gifted Polish poet Wislawa Szymborska told her esteemed audience in Stockholm:

. . . in daily speech, where we don't stop to consider every word, we all use phrases such as "the ordinary world", "ordinary life", "the ordinary course of events". But in the language of poetry, where every word is weighed, nothing is usual or normal. Not a single stone and not a single cloud above it. Not a single day and

not a single night after it. And above all, not a single
existence, not anyone's existence in this world. It looks
as though poets will always have their work cut out for
them.[27]

We do well to learn from the mother whale as she warned her
baby whale: 'Be careful, my dear, for it is when you are
spouting that you are most likely to get harpooned.' The poetic
Church will know how to measure its verbal output and when
to keep silence. Philip Larkin once criticised a new form of jazz
music which strove 'after something that isn't there, ie to
move the listener by adopting the idiom which cannot move
you in the least'.[28] Whilst it is not the place to enter the
liturgical debate any further, I would hope that liturgies in
the future will not find themselves similarly sterile because of
an initial lack of poetic determination. Or, in Wittgenstein's
clear image, because of a failure to remember that 'a wheel
that can be turned though nothing else moves with it, is not
part of the mechanism'.

It is my hope that the Church's liturgies and her words will,
like the bells of Venice in a novel by James Cowan, grasp us
and begin to transform our understanding for the sake of the
eternal: 'The sound of St Mark's bells pealing across the water
at dusk is less the sound of clappers against brass . . . it is the
echo of an invitation being extended to all of us to participate
in something deeply imagined'.[29]

It is only then that we will be able to fully agree with Les
Murray that

Full religion is the large poem in loving repetition . . .
. . . and God is the poetry caught in any religion,
caught, not imprisoned. Caught as in a mirror
that he attracted, being in the world as poetry is in
the poem, a law against closure.[30]

part two
COMPOSITION

four
TRUTHFULNESS

What's known but ignored takes its revenge . . .

Martha Cooley

Explanations must be as simple as possible – and no simpler.

Albert Einstein

The borrowed truths are the ones to which one clings most tenaciously, and all the more since they remain foreign to our most intimate self.

André Gide

In his novel *Miss Smilla's Feeling for Snow* the Danish author Peter Hoeg creates a character who is able to work out a human being's age, background, geography and education from his or her accent. His friend is amazed at this skill. How does he do it? 'I was originally a theologian,' he replies, 'an occupation that presents excellent opportunities for listening to people.'[1]

The belief that those who are concerned to seek the reality

of God must be good listeners is one I hold very strongly. 'If words are not things,' wrote Coleridge, 'they are living powers, by which the things of most importance are actuated, combined and humanized'. Through listening to each other's words we deepen our awareness of each other, the worlds which it is possible to inhabit, the truths which necessarily contribute to our own understanding of Truth. We are living in a world more attracted to information than communication, more comfortable with facts than with meaning, more ready to describe what is than what should be. Making meaning today is hard. We are confronted by a swarm of conflicting vocabularies, like angry bees, that relate rival accounts (religious, political, psychological) of human nature and destiny. There is at the same time considerable distrust of these public languages and this is cause for concern because, as Czeslaw Milosz knew from his own experience in postwar Poland, 'men will clutch at illusions when they have nothing else to hold to'.[2]

As one of these public discourses, the Christian faith need not, I would argue, be threatened by the present multiplication of voices. Dietrich Bonhoeffer was well aware of the dangerous implications of some ideologies but was still able to believe that 'Christianity puts us into many different dimensions of life at the same time; we make room in ourselves, to some extent, for God and the whole world . . . Life is kept multi-dimensional and polyphonous. What a deliverance it is to think, and thereby to remain multi-dimensional'.[3]

This seems to me to be vitally obvious but it needs to be said again and again, especially when many Christian approaches, both doctrinal and social, are currently urging their own to huddle together in a cold climate, like the mad clergyman who locked his church and filled the pews with a congregation of cardboard cut-outs. As I write, some parts of the Church do not seem to have much energy for engaged debate, implying that to be in the right mind you cannot have an open one. Truth quickly takes on a private, rather than a public, nature.

To live within such a comfortable but small house, not allowing outsiders to approach the front door or even to question your taste in furniture, is a way of life that is ultimately working for exclusion and self-approval in uncertain days. At its worst, it becomes a sort of religious fascism, unable to celebrate diversity and brutally working for order and purity.

Negotiation for the sake of grace was Bonhoeffer's preferred alternative. As Carolyn M. Jones has shown, his habit was to face what was unknown by him and to understand it on indigenous terms as far as possible in order to let it adjust his own horizons. He made the often difficult journey to the margins in order to see the centre from the edges and, if need be, to relocate it:

> I see . . . Bonhoeffer sitting in his prison cell, pen in hand. I am always amazed that, as he faced death, he did not give up hope or retreat into the security of religious systems or his own ego. Imprisoned in a few feet of space, he tore down walls . . .[4]

Bonhoeffer was not an anarchist out to destroy Christian faith. Far from it. He was a disciple of faith, not certainty, and as such sought out the God of the universe in all the places he came across in which he might be hidden.

In today's world, one way in which we are able to tear down some of our own imprisoning walls is to enter into the world of narrative. Every novel is a voice, a world, displaying a pattern of relationships and inner landscapes. People of faith, on the journey towards seeing more of the great richness of God each day, can enlarge their picture of the world, and their own place in it, by a dialogue with other human beings and their various arts.

John Dagenais, in his work *The Ethics of Reading in Manuscript Culture*,[5] calls the reading that was typical in medieval Europe *lecturature*, that is, reading that is also composition. *Lecturature* is not engaged principally in amassing information or developing literary style. It is done to change the reader's thinking, emotional and active life. This is achieved by ingestion and rumination resulting in a translation and creation within the reader. This active reading is not the consumerist, and somewhat promiscuous, reading that the speed of today forces us into all too often. It is artful, measured and alert. George Steiner's reflections on Chardin's painting *Le Philosophe Lisant*[6] note that the reader in the painting is literally dressed for the occasion and does not meet the book casually. There is almost a courtly display towards the text in front of him, similar to that of a Talmudic scholar who 'seeks the flame of the spirit in the fixity of the letter'. Steiner reveals that an exchange is taking place between the reader and the text. Both are being read by the other. New worlds are being explored.

Christians have no orthodoxy but that of truth. It is our duty to unearth it wherever it may lie, no matter how uncomfortable its presence may be. Unfortunately, because we have been so used to committing ourselves to systems of belief, often fine-tuned but always inevitably historically conditioned, we find it awkward to face new truth. There have been many victims throughout the years who have suffered at the hands of intransigent and proud Christian thinking. Galileo comes to mind, as do the huge numbers of martyrs from the Reformation period, but there are many more people who have been, and still are, badly bruised or worse by the destructive fear that is often crouching amongst the elegant grasses of tidy theological gardens. 'Man,' reflects Dostoyevsky in his *Notes from Underground*, 'has such a predilection for systems and abstract deductions that he is ready to distort the truth intentionally, he is ready to deny the evidence of his sense in order to justify his logic'.

Systems of thought are the subordination of all the aspects of the universe to one of those approaches. As Bonhoeffer realised, nothing could be more artificial and controlling than

such an imposition on God. R.S. Thomas also understands the
narrowness of such thinking:

> You have made God small,
> setting him astride
> a pipette or a retort
> studying the bubbles,
> absorbed in an experiment
> that will come to nothing.
>
> I think of him rather
> as an enormous owl
> abroad in the shadows,
> brushing me sometimes
> with his wing so the blood
> in my veins freezes, able
>
> to find his way from one
> soul to another because
> he can see in the dark.
> I have heard him crooning
> to himself, so that almost
> I could believe in angels,
>
> those feathered overtones
> in love's rafters, I have heard
> him scream, too, fastening
> his talons in his great adversary,
> or in some lesser
> denizen, maybe, like you or me.[7]

Because I believe God 'can see in the dark', and for the other
reasons I have already mentioned, I lament very much the fact
that the word 'liberal' has become almost unusable in the
contemporary Church. The word is shadowed by the image of

clapped-out angst-ridden clergy in cardigans who 'don't believe much' any more. It is also soiled by what might be called the illiberal liberals, who are unable to tolerate those who do not share their more radical views.

In contrast to both these images, I see the need for a renewed spirit of liberality in the Church, a spirit concerned to ensure that the Church keeps a breadth of mind, a general courtesy in its communal life, a desire to defend another's right of speech and interpretation of shared texts, and maintains a greater concern to check its own prejudices than preserve its so-called 'purity'. A person only need spend a short time reflecting on how he or she has changed views throughout his or her life so far, and think about how they may change again in the future, to realise that the Church should be able to hold all this within – and much more as well.

Such liberality, in contradistinction to the religious fascism I mentioned earlier, will celebrate diversity and be unashamed of a necessary pluriformity regarding differing views on certain controversial topics. It will celebrate the generous liberality of God towards his creation and encourage Christian people to awaken themselves to the memory of the Church by being transparent to its origin and to the necessity of praying together, and it will seek an ordered life in those it ordains and entrusts with its various ministries. It will encourage questioning, enquiry and debate. It will know that a sentence always means more and will have *'le courage de nos différences'*. In short, it will be unafraid to reason and unashamed to adore. Its purpose will be to transform, with the grace of God, human memory, understanding and will into faith, hope and love. To this end, a true Christian liberality will be more concerned to direct our limited language to God rather than about God. Liberality can only be authentic, and not narcissistic, if it is born in a patient waiting on the outpouring of God in prayer. Only then can its own temptations to power and pride be confronted. All speech about the Holy One is costly for it demands penitence of us at each and every turn.

Christian liberality will never be defined by how a person votes in this or that debate. 'Many who think themselves emancipated are merely unbuttoned'.[8] It is more a matter of the approach to the debate and to those others taking part. It is a *procedural* liberalism more than a *substantive* liberalism that will hold us together. We tend to find such generosity and encouragement a positive element in an individual, say in a teacher or friend. We find it harder to appreciate in an organisation, such is its power to draw us into its search for control: 'Pitted against our capacity for empathy is a craving for regimentation'.[9]

Christian liberality, then, is essential if we are to make friendships amongst our own Christian communities and with those outside them. It does not mean a free for all and a disregard for authority. An informal attitude towards our tradition is nothing less than arrogant. Theology is like sewing: you need to knot the thread. It means allowing room for growth and change in individual hearts and minds, and in the Church's life and faith as embodied in the years that pass. It will never just simply be the Church's roots that give it shape and allow it to continue on; it will be the liberal and generous momentum of the whole organism which will permit it adventure, branching out and allowing more birds, of different shapes and sizes, to nest in its leaves. The sooner we stop feeling embarrassed by this the better.

In Iris Murdoch's *Henry and Cato* we are told by the story's priest that he sometimes feels that one day he might receive some perfect illumination about absolutely everything but he knows that this is an illusion and that 'the point is one will never get to the end of it, never get to the bottom of it, never, never. And that never, never, never is what you must take for your hope and your shield and your most glorious promise'.[10]

The search for truth, then, can be entered into by Christians with a great variety of people, not least novelists, and it can be surprising with whom one finds oneself talking. Franz Kafka wrote to his friend Oskar Pollak in 1904 offering some thoughts on reading:

> I think we ought to read only the kind of books that wound and stab us . . . We need the books that affect us like a disaster, that grieve us deeply, like the death of someone we loved more than ourselves, like being banished into forests far from everyone, like a suicide. A book must be the axe for the frozen sea inside us.[11]

The novels of Ian McEwan, for instance, may not have been the first choice of some to enlighten them. Early on in his career McEwan made a name for himself as being dark and unpleasantly off track, and hence he was quickly nicknamed 'Ian Macabre'. The BBC refused to produce his play *Solid Geometry* on the grounds of its supposed obscenity. He has mastered the art beautifully caught in the description 'épater les bourgeois' (shake or shock middle-class attitudes). He raises the axe over the frozen sea. However, he is also a master of detection, a spy on human peculiarities and practices and his writing digs around the deep shadowed caves of the human mind. A sense of his interests can be caught in a poem by W.H. Auden:

At last the secret is out, as it always must come in the end
The delicious story is ripe to tell to the intimate friend;
Over the tea cups and in the square the tongue has its desire;
Still waters run deep, my dear, there's never smoke without
    fire.

Behind the corpse in the reservoir, behind the ghost on the
    links,
Behind the lady who dances and the man who madly drinks,
Under the look of fatigue, the attack of migraine and the sigh

There is always another story, there is more than meets the
   eye.

For the clear voice suddenly singing, high up in the convent
   wall,
The scent of the elder bushes, the sporting prints in the hall,
The croquet matches in summer, the handshake, the cough,
   the kiss
There is always a wicked secret, a private reason for this.[12]

The apparently innocent signs by which people unwittingly
give away hints of what is hidden allow McEwan to identify
secrets which would otherwise not be released. As a Christian
priest and pastor I share his interest: not because I am a
frisky priest instead of a whisky one, but because daily pastoral
work reveals to me that, like old vases, human beings have
mended cracks that only become visible close up. The wounds
and the secrets are the places where healing is received or
rejected. Pastors who prefer the bloodless sentimentalisation of
religion to the unseen depths from which people cry with tears
or with joy are not consecrating themselves in truth.

Nabokov once said that the inspiration for his book *Lolita*
came from a newspaper story about a keeper at the Paris zoo
who trained an ape to draw. The first recognisable picture the
animal produced was of the bars of its cage. Nabokov likewise
sought to draw in his writing the bars of the human cage. Such
explorations are vital for the human spirit as it splashes about
taking deep gulps of air. Only those who know their need for
such air will hear the piercing words which promise to the
heavy laden and distressed a gentleness of heart, a calming of
the storm, a crossing to the other side. Such words are not
made for anodyne greetings cards, they are addressed to the
deepest human recognitions and will. Christian faith is not
sanctified common sense. It concerns itself with the full spectrum of reality as experienced by men and women through

history. Theology needs to admit chaos and to find a form that accommodates the mess we encounter. Richard Sheridan's biographer says of her subject that 'no-one could throw a veil of meaningless phrase over awkward truth more skilfully'. We need to be careful that, in some sort of attempt to protect God or the Church, we don't end up doing the same in a discipleship that is intended to lead us into all truth.

In McEwan's novel *Amsterdam*, colleagues find photographs of Garmony, the Foreign Secretary, dressed in women's clothing. The author comments:

> We know so little about each other. We lie mostly submerged like ice floes, with our visible social selves projecting only cool and white. Here was a rare sight below the waves, of a man's privacy and turmoil, of his dignity upended by the overpowering necessity of pure thought, by the irreducible human element – mind.[13]

McEwan's art of unease shows us the sights below the waves and reveals the places where the subterranean fight for redemption might be fought. I believe that those called to a Christian ministry with other people also know the necessity of developing the arts of unease which disturb the complacencies and armours we live with. Reading McEwan's novels is a good example of how the Christian might search more adventurously for human truth. W.H. Auden, particularly in his Christmas Oratorio *For the Time Being*, similarly knew that the shameful elements of life can be embraced within a redemptive vision. As the title of Eleanor Bron's autobiography – *Life and other Punctures*[14] – suggests, the world is not always as convenient as we would like.

Christianity is not concerned for sugar and spice and all things nice. It requires imaginative courage to face the darkness, and also to suffer one's confusion, so that it can be met with Christ's light. It is a case of being open to the world as it is for the sake of the world to come. Something of this is, I believe, found in Laurence Whistler's engraved church window where Judas is portrayed with a rope around his neck. He is being pulled into heaven and, as he is slowly raised, the coins of betrayal are seen falling from his hands, transformed into petals and flowers on the ground. Theology can be as daring in its thoughts as this because the arena is properly God's. Describing humanity's immense glory and failure, Pascal asked: 'Who will unravel such a tangle? This is certainly beyond dogmatism and scepticism, beyond all human philosophy . . .'[15]

A good example of a rigorous theological project is the late Medieval Mystery Plays which, according to Auerbach, achieved a shift in the Western representation of reality:

> This great drama contains everything that occurs in world history . . . all the heights and depths of human conduct and all the heights and depths of stylistic expression . . . there is no basis for a separation of the sublime from the low and everyday, for they are indissolubly connected in Christ's very life and suffering. Nor is there any basis for the concern for the unities of time, place or action, for there is but one place – the world; and one action – man's fall and redemption.[16]

As I get older, the world gets more complex and layered for me. McEwan and many other novelists are unafraid to reveal this world where rules are difficult to discern, voices can be hollow and the villain often avoids detection: *cucullus non facit monachum*.[17] We live with existential anxieties of having failed to become oneself and, also, of having become oneself. To break such anxiety will require an understanding of it. To suffer one's own ingredients can be the first step towards healing. For instance, it has taken me a long time to learn that those who love to be feared are the ones who often have the fear of being loved. I now see that such an understanding has the potential to unlock infinite possibilities: 'And yet. Those are my two favourite words, applicable to every situation, be it happy or bleak'.[18]

The world is also being investigated by scientists in ways we could never have imagined only a few years ago. Similarly, those who have faith in the creative God must have an openness of mind about new discoveries and the interpretative models utilised to contextualise them.

In placing the threads of heaven into an integrated tapestry, we will need to be truthful no matter what the cost. It will often involve enormous independence of spirit for, as Descartes declared, 'the assent of many voices is not a valid proof for truths'. To acknowledge our own need and poverty is the beginning of truthfulness for much pain is borne in the knowledge that some secrets seem fated never to be revealed.

We are not purveyors of ready-made meaning. This commitment to truth, as pilgrims rather than arrivals, is what allows us to confess that as Christians, even Christian leaders, we are first and foremost explorers rather than illustrators. As Simone Weil argued consistently in her various books, the need of truth is more sacred than any other need.

Some medieval maps used to warn travellers of uncharted waters by solemnly including the words 'where unknown, there place monsters'. In the search for truth and wisdom the Christian is likely to be more adventurous and write with a different signature:

>   about
>   catastrophe or how to behave in one
>   what do I know, except what everyone knows –
>   if there when Grace dances, I should dance.[19]

Alfred Kerr, in his biography of Henrik Ibsen published in 1905, summarised the artist's contribution to the world that was so often shocked at the topics he raised. Ibsen was well aware that truth more than often resides on the reverse side of what is familiarly known. I have wondered whether Christian faith might learn something from Kerr's conclusion:

> The best and most momentous things that Ibsen has given us are the impulse to truth in an artistically untruthful time; the impulse to seriousness in an artistically super-ficial time; the pleasure of agitation in a time of stagnation; and the courage to grasp whatever contains something human, wherever it grows.[20]

five
PRAYING

The God-shaken, in whom is the truth inborn.

T.S. Eliot

To clasp the hands in prayer is the beginning of an
uprising against the disorder of the world.

Karl Barth

Unless you find Paradise
at your centre,
there is not the smallest chance
that you may enter

Angelus Silesius

T he story is told of three clergy who, while having a drink in the pub one evening, were discussing the problem each of them had with bats in their churches. The first said that he had tried to entice them out but it had not worked. There were still hundreds of them in his belfry. The second explained that a control company had been brought in but nothing had changed. There were still bats everywhere. Then the third priest spoke up: 'I've got rid of all mine,' he said. 'How on earth have you done that?' the other two asked eagerly. 'I just baptised and confirmed them all,' he replied, 'and I never saw them again.'

As the story suggests, it is well known that many people fall away somewhat from their initial commitment to the Christian faith. Sociologists and theologians alike have worked hard in trying to find answers as to why this occurs. At the same time, various surveys in the United Kingdom reveal that a large majority of people are willing to say that they believe in a personal God and that they regularly pray. No further questions are usually asked as to what they mean by prayer or how they go about it. It seems generally accepted to refer to a request, or maybe a thanksgiving, offered up to an all-knowing and all-powerful God who might influence events in the future on the supplicant's behalf.

There are many Christian people who would agree with such a conception of prayer; and there are those, like me, who are unhappy with it. At the same time, I would want to argue that prayer is the most important part of the collage of faith, indeed you might even say that it is the glue with which the collage is being pieced together. It seems necessary then to try and describe what it is I mean when I use the word 'prayer'.

The popular view of prayer I have just mentioned is bound up with an image of God's power. Power, in this framework, is understood as control, strength and absolute ability. It follows that if God wanted to make us all good, feed the hungry in Africa and even, perhaps, make a square circle, he could. He chooses not to and instead grants us free will but, as a father, listens and responds to our prayers as he sees fit. This is a poor snapshot of the conception of prayer that some hold but, with slight variations here and there, it is something along these lines that describes some people's belief in prayer today. If there are no such possibilities of influencing the future, they continue, why bother to pray in the first place?

Robert Pinsky, in his essay on 'The Responsibilities of the Poet', claims that an artist:

> . . . needs not so much an audience, as to feel a need to answer, a promise to respond. The promise may be a contradiction, it may be unwanted, it may go unheeded . . . but it is owed, and the sense that it is owed is a basic requirement for the poet's good feeling about the art. This need to answer, as firm as a borrowed object or a cash debt, is the ground where the centaur walks.[1]

Finding oneself breathing in a world of gift and promise can, for some, demand such 'a need to answer, a promise to respond' to the giver and origin of life itself:

> Listening deeply, man kept faith with
> the source.[2]

The impulse to pray can be of such notable force that it is unignorable. It is a response to the wonder, the darkness and the discovery within a life on this earth. It is therefore as acquainted with what Virgil termed the *lacrimae rerum*, the tears of things, as it is with the raising of the heart in gratitude. The acknowledgement of this gift of limited time on earth is found quite often in Szymborska's poetry:

> Nothing's a gift, it's all on loan.
> I'm drowning in debts up to my ears.
> I'll have to pay for myself
> with my self,
> give up my life for my life.
>
> Here's how it's arranged:
> The heart can be repossessed,
> the liver, too,
> and each single finger and toe.

Too late to tear up the terms,
my debts will be repaid,
and I'll be fleeced,
or, more precisely, flayed.

I move about the planet
in a crush of other debtors.
Some are saddled with the burden
of paying off their wings.
Others must, willy-nilly,
account for every leaf.

Every tissue in us lies
on the debit side.
Not a tentacle or tendril
is for keeps.

The inventory, infinitely detailed,
implies we'll be left
not just empty-handed
but handless, too.

I can't remember
where, when, and why
I let someone open
this account in my name.

We call the protest against this
the soul.
And it's the only item
not included on the list.[3]

The protest against all disintegration is the soul and prayer, as
George Herbert saw it, is 'the soul in paraphrase'.[4] Prayer is
first and foremost the response of the created self towards the

eternity of its creator. It is the recognition that we are dependent beings, limited, exposed and frail. Prayer beckons us out
of ourselves and awakens in us our longing for the Holy and
Eternal One. The tenth-century St Symeon invites us to
imagine:

> . . . a man standing at night inside his house with all the
> doors closed: and then suppose that he opens a window
> just at the moment when there is a sudden flash of light-
> ening. Unable to bear its brightness, at once he protects
> himself by closing his eyes and drawing back from the
> window. So it is with the soul that is enclosed in the realm
> of the senses: if ever she peeps out through the window of
> the mind, she is overwhelmed by the brightness, like
> lightning, of the pledge of the Holy Spirit that is within
> her. Unable to bear the splendour of unveiled light, at
> once she is bewildered in her mind, and she draws back
> entirely upon herself, taking refuge as in a house, among
> sensory and human things. [5]

The ancient Assyrians used the same word for prayer as for the
act of unclenching a fist. If we think how often in a day we have
our fist clenched we begin to see the importance of this image
of prayer. The clenched fist, as depicted for instance in the film
Remains of the Day, can represent so much of the human spirit –
high-handedness, pride, threatening behaviour, possessiveness,
control. People use clenched fists to assault others and hurt
them. Prayer, however, in the spirit of Christ who prayed for
his Father's will to be done, is a renouncing of such attitudes.
As the soul awakens so the fists unfold. To open our hands to
God is to reject violence, pride and a belief in our self-
sufficiency. Open hands form an invitation to the future to take
shape as the will of God directs it. Our hands were empty at
our birth, we have received everything as gift and, as people
who try to keep our hands uncluttered, we venture every day
to give voice to our dependence on God and offer them to his

service. As portrayed so beautifully in Michelangelo's famous painting of the making of Adam on the ceiling of the Sistine Chapel, where God and humanity both stretch out towards one another, the energy of God awakens people out of non-existence, it brings newness each day, and freshness in stillness.

There is a famous story of St Kevin, the Irish monk, who, it is said, was kneeling in prayer one day in the fields of Glendalough with his arms outstretched in the form of a cross. A blackbird mistook his hand for a roost and laid a clutch of eggs in it, as if she were on a branch of a tree. With his deep love for wildlife, Kevin stayed immobile for weeks on end holding out his hand until the eggs hatched and the fledglings grew wings.

This story holds together, in true Celtic spirit, the natural process with the glimpsed ideal. It is 'at one and the same time a signpost and a reminder'[6] of the possibilities that lie in the open spirit tuning itself on God. In *The Silver Spoon*, when John Galsworthy describes Fleur's fourteen-month-old son, Kit, taking a bath with 'kicks and crows and splashings', he comments that the small boy was giving thanks 'not for what he was about to receive, but for what he was receiving'.[7] Prayer is similarly focused: becoming like a child for the sake of the Kingdom of Heaven.

Compare this to a preoccupied view of prayer amusingly exposed by Wendy Cope:

> When I went out shopping,
> I said a little prayer:
> 'Jesus, help me park the car
> For you are everywhere.'
>
> *Jesus, in His goodness and grace,*
> *Jesus found me a parking space*
> *In a very convenient place.*
> *Sound the horn and praise Him!*

His eternal car-park
Is hidden from our eyes.
Trust in Him and you will have
A space beyond the skies.

Jesus, in His goodness and grace,
Wants to find you a parking space.
Ask Him now to reserve a place.
Sound the horn and praise Him![8]

Naturally, as the human being comes before God in prayer he or she brings all that is on the mind and heart. We have genuine and sincere concerns, not just for ourselves but for those we love and are fond of. We can also find ourselves upset, anxious or angry about situations in the wider world and carry these around with us too. Once again the image of the opening fist is helpful. For if we think that prayer is more akin to a clenched fist banging down its demands, we have become proud enough to believe that our limited visions and understandings must be shared by God and that he should empower them with his mighty hand in bringing them to effect. To pray to such a God is not to pray to the God revealed in the silence, trust and heartache of the cross. The good news of the gospel of Christ is the celebration of life, salvation and hope discovered when the will of God is worked for and manifested in unselfish lives. It is not magic. It is following the one who laid down his life for his friends.

To pray for others is to commend them to God, to seek his blessing and provision. It is also an attending to our own responsibilities. Prayer is never a substitute for human action. It is where we fight for the freedom of our vision and love:

He prays unceasingly who combines prayer with necessary duties and duties with prayer. Only in this way can we find it practicable to fulfil the commandment to pray always. It consists in regarding the whole of Christian existence as a single great prayer. What we are accustomed to call prayer is only a part of it.[9]

It is giving loving attention to the nature of things, to the world and loved ones in it. It is also to correct the corruptions of human power:

> To pray is to place oneself in the silent presence of the Eternal Beyond, the God of Truth and Love, and letting the flow of communication between that and one's truest self clarify the distorted vision, purify the motives, countervail the pressures and set one free from dependence upon any other power except the care for others which holds on, trusting, hoping and enduring, until in the long term it wins through.[10]

In the marvellous recent production of Tony Harrison's Mystery Plays[11] at the Cottesloe Theatre, God was seen at the top of a large iron mast creating the world. As he called out the names of the sea, land, plants and creatures, so strips of coloured material with outlines of these new forms unfurled from him and were held out for all to see. When all the strips were complete, a band struck up and the mast and materials were transformed into a May pole. Holding the cloths, men and women danced around, under the loving grin of their creator, weaving in and out and displaying the dark shades and bright flashes in a riotous pattern of movement. On the two nights I saw this performance the audience unselfconsciously stood up and began to jig around and clap their hands, trying to find their own place in this extraordinary event. On the stage-level people even began to join in the dance with the actors and we saw tired after-work businessmen in suits, children excited at still being up and seeing their parents make a fool of themselves, giggling women from the office, the whole spectrum of a London audience – gay, straight, elderly, young, rich and unemployed – all finding a place, straightening their postures for the music and hoping the dance would go on into the night. It was a true liturgy for the human spirit, and as we bopped around and clapped, the actor playing God slowly outstretched his arms over us all in blessing, willing us to carry on but, as his arms remained there, we also saw the form of a cross. His love that night, we knew, was both celebration and anguish. The music played on.

It seems to me that the one who prays is engaged in the business of finding his or her place in this divine dance of grace. We carry with us so much as we try to keep whirling in and out. To see all that is necessary for the dance to be lighter is to glimpse prayer. Sometimes, like some of the mums at the performance carrying their tired children, we need to carry others as we struggle to find our footing and hear the harmonies. We were never meant to dance for ourselves only. When we lift up, and hold tight, of those who do not have the energy to play their part, we begin to resemble the One who carries us. Intercession enables the music to play on. By praying for people Alan Ecclestone said he learned 'to see our personal lives not as pitiful threads soon to be snapped and forgotten – but as threads woven into an amazing tapestry of life. To pray is to try and extend that emotion, to come back to it, and to deepen it. This practice teaches us indebtedness.'[12]

Because prayer is a relationship of presence we can often feel frustrated when there appears to be no presence of God with us and we can be tempted to abandon the exercise. Those who have known lives of prayer have disciplined themselves into necessary routines in order that our response to God is not simply based on our changeable moods and feelings. Those who enter the depths of a prayerful encounter with God have also experienced the darkness and doubts that any relationship knows only too well. Relationships are forged and crafted through time; they move in and out of different ways of being, and they suffer if they try to imitate others too closely. Our prayer with God breathes the same air:

> First forgive the silence
> > That answers prayer,
> Then forgive the prayer
> > That stains the silence.
> Excuse the absence
> > That feels like presence,
> Then excuse the feeling
> > That insists on presence.
> Pardon the delay
> > Of revelation,
> Then ask pardon for revealing
> > Your impatience.
> Forgive God
> > For being only a word
> Then ask God to forgive
> > The betrayal of language.[13]

The physical impatience that prefers the cult of fitness to health is related to the spiritual restlessness that demands signs and the extraordinary. There is so much inside us that seeks freedom that we look for confirmation that we have it. We resist ourselves, who we've been and who we've become. The tension of this resistance enters our bodies and incorporates itself into us. It is no wonder that we finally tire. 'Nothing in all creation is so like God as stillness,' reminded Meister Eckhart and it is through the reflections of God, given to us in prayer, that such stillness filters into us and we find our home away from the noise and distraction. When Kierkegaard wondered why Jesus showed little anxiety in the face of his forthcoming arrest and trial he concluded: 'It was because he had eternity with him in the day that is called today: hence the next day had no power over him, it had no existence for him.'[14]

R.S. Thomas entitled one of his collections of poetry *Experimenting With an Amen*. A prayerful individual and a prayerful church will know the hazards and rewards of such experimentation. An open-handed body of Christian people, not concerned with power as much as making God's presence known, will offer words of longing, thanksgiving, intercession and questioning. In all this 'the meaning is in the waiting'[15] and encouragement is enough:

> Prayers like gravel
>   Flung at the sky's
> window, hoping to attract
>   the loved one's
> attention. But without
>   visible plaits to let
> down for the believer
>   to climb up,
> to what purpose open
>   that far casement?
>   I would
> have refrained long since
>   but that peering once
> through my locked fingers
> I thought that I detected
>   the movement of a curtain.[16]

six
SERVICE

*If your morals make you dreary, depend upon it,
they are wrong.*

Robert Louis Stevenson

Love proves itself by constant renewal.

Alan Hollinghurst

*Never look down to test the ground before taking
your next step: only he who keeps his eye on the far
horizon will find his right road.*

Dag Hammarskjold

The average person's attention span today is incredibly limited. For this reason, makers of TV programmes and films create short scenes and, if possible, pack them with action, noise and intrigue to maintain the viewer's interest. They know that it is only too easy for that viewer to change channel at the push of a button or to turn to some other form of entertainment altogether.

For this reason, the success of a film made in the late eighties by Gabriel Axel, and starring Stephane Audran, might be thought a little puzzling. However, *Babette's Feast* won many awards and hearts for its translation onto the screen of a story by Karen Blixen, otherwise known as Isak Dinesen. It moves at a slow pace and has minimal dialogue. By taking this form it captures the spirit of the original narrative and teases us to touch the various meanings and implications that dance around in the story.

Babette's Feast,[1] one of the author's later works, was first published in the *Ladies Home Journal* in the United States in 1950. Karen Blixen, though, was Danish, and it is in the North that we find ourselves at the beginning of a tale which, I believe, may be read as a parable by those of us who are searching how to embody in life the faith we profess in words. Let me briefly recount the outline of the story which was set in the late nineteenth century.

Two elderly sisters live together in a remote village. Their late father had been a minister of a hard-line ascetic religious community and his memory is still reverenced by the villagers. The sisters spend their days in prayer and charitable work until, one stormy night, a distressed woman arrives at their door with a letter from a friend of theirs in Paris. The letter explains that events back home, due to the Franco-Prussian war, are so bad that Babette has fled. Her husband and son have already been killed. The letter informs the women that he has told her to make her way to them as he feels sure that they will both find a place for her in their home – perhaps as a servant. The sisters tell Babette that, unfortunately, they do not have the money to pay her but Babette offers to work without any payment: 'If I cannot,' she says, 'I will die.'

So, Babette works for them for fourteen years until, one day, she receives a letter from a friend in Paris who has been looking after her lottery ticket. She has won ten thousand francs, which is an enormous amount of money. On hearing of this, the sisters have mixed feelings because they realise that Babette is sure to leave them now as she owns such a fortune.

At the same time, the sisters have been planning a gathering in their home to commemorate their late father. Babette now asks them if she may be permitted to cook a Parisian meal for them and their friends and to pay for it herself out of her newly acquired money. The sisters object, but Babette reminds them that she has never asked anything of them before and so, eventually, they agree.

Puritanical Christians are suspicious of the human senses and luxuries and the villagers, although admitting that it is kind of Babette to cook for them, decide to be silent about the meal and to behave as if they have no taste. Babette knows nothing of this as she carefully makes out her shopping lists and the large crates arrive from France safe and sound.

On the evening of the meal, a visiting general happens to be in the town and is invited along to the meal. As the guests take their seats around a sumptuously laid table, with cut glass and fine linens, and as they then begin to eat the exquisite turtle soup and drink the fantastic amontillado sherry, the general becomes aware that this food and wine is of the highest quality and has obviously been prepared by someone highly skilled. In fact, he says to the otherwise quiet guests, this dinner reminds him of one he once had in the Café Anglais, one which had been created by the head chef. We later discover that this had been Babette when she worked in Paris.

Later in the meal, after a glass or two, the villagers begin to loosen up and begin talking to one another. Things start to happen. Two old women, for instance, who have been slandering one another suddenly recall the days of their childhood when they had made their way together to confirmation class hand in hand. Their memories reconcile them. Two businessmen make up after a long-standing disagreement and, perhaps most touching, a man and woman finally admit their love for one another and seal it with a small kiss. The table which has been prepared so lovingly becomes a place of reconciliation and celebration.

After the dinner, when the guests have gone home, the sisters go into the kitchen and find the exhausted Babette surrounded by pots and pans and they thank her for doing such a marvellous deed before leaving them. Babette tells them that she is not leaving. Besides, she has no money. The sisters are confused. Why doesn't she have any money? Where is all her lottery money? Babette tells them simply that she spent it all on the dinner. She has nothing left. She was given an opportunity to do the best she could and that was enough for her. The two sisters weep for joy and embrace her which, again, was something that had never happened before.

I believe this story can be read as a parable for in it one cannot fail to see the Christ figure in Babette. She arrives unexpectedly and although great becomes a servant and, as she says, if they stop her being a servant she will surely die (echoes of a cross?). We are told by the author that for fourteen years all the two sisters want Babette to cook is fish and bread, the ordinary diet of poor northern Europeans. Babette, however, dreams and then prepares a banquet where what is offered surprises the guests and where there is plenty for everyone. At this banquet memories are brought out and reconciled. The future is given hope as the layers of protective pain slip away. One might even say that the blind begin to see again and the lame leap. All are being made alive in a new creation. In fact, in the film, as the guests make their way home they link arms and have a little jig down the road. One senses that their tomorrows have been transformed.

Babette's action is selfless but skilful. She spends herself and is broken so that all might receive from her goodness. And then, at the end, exhausted and poor, she completes her love and her art. The sisters ask her to stay with them, just as those disciples did on the road to Emmaus when they too had recognised truth in the breaking of bread.

Dinesen's story needs to be revisited today for it alerts us to the concept of serving our neighbour and the creation of personhood. When Disraeli was told that the radical John Bright had a humble background and was an entirely self-made man, he answered: 'I know he is — and he adores his maker too.' The idea that as individuals we are self-made is one of the most damaging, and yet persuasive, of our present time. It can also encourage a pride in us which inhibits our capacity to connect with those we share life with.

We are not self-made. We receive our life and breath as a gift; we are shaped and moulded by the people and circumstances that touch us through our lives. We are woven with varied threads and so often the colours are brought to us and are not of our own making. Those who follow the Christian way know that we are members one of another and that, as fragile creatures in the making, we need to be careful, gentle and discerning of each other. We can both help someone to burst into flower or we can badly bruise, even destroy, them.

In the Gospel of St John, Jesus calls his disciples friends rather than servants.[2] It has always perplexed me that, as a Church, we do not spend much energy on reflecting through the sacred benefits of friendship. We tend, instead, to place it in the context of endless talk about sexual relationships, a topic on which we too often create more heat than light. It is undeniable, though, that our lives can be deepened and broadened in the company of good friends and that the life-enhancing character of such friendship may reveal something of the God who calls us to befriend him:

> Oh, the comfort, the inexpressible comfort, of feeling safe with a person; having neither to weigh thoughts, nor measure words, but pour them all out, just as they are, chaff and grain together, knowing that a faithful hand will take and sift them, keep what is worth keeping, and then, with a breath of kindness, blow the rest away.[3]

Various turbulent points in our lives are charged with emotions, traditionally as we relate, first, to parents and then lovers. The human path towards identity feels at first as if it should be taken alone but, to our initial irritation, we find others placed there without our asking. When love comes along a little later, we wonder how it might be possible to keep our identity and, at the same time, live for another person.

The complications and frustrations of existing *for* others, with its dutiful responsibilities and frequently damaging ideal role models, begin to level for many of us as we get older and turn to the equally challenging business of living *with* others. Friendship is the perfecting of this latter art. To become a friend we have somehow to remain equal with another, levelling ourselves so that we can look face to face. There is something distinctly unpretentious about true friendship and, as such, it is possible to discover the identity we have been shaping in another's acceptance of our own freedom.

Not only can we depend on a friend but we become someone upon whom others depend. The promise to walk together is the first rule of friendship, rooting the relationship in faithfulness. Nothing can reveal the poverty of the belief that we are self-made than having a true friend to share life with. Friendship is not a simply passive relationship, though. It can be confrontational too. It is the friend who can spot our own destructive traits, forced upon ourselves or others, and who will urge us to resist these and draw on what is positive and enriching within us instead. It can be so easy to believe that I am the one who should have all the attention and to feel rejected when that attention isn't given. A friend replaces this anxiety in our centre and our obsessive self-focusing. A friend is able to draw us out of ourselves and teach us how to celebrate all the things we have been missing because of our narrowness. It can be startling to find out who can be such a friend. It may be a partner, parent or child. It may be someone hugely different from us, someone who meets us from a distance.

The dynamics of friendship may alert us to the energies of God. We receive life from him and, as those he creates, gradually learn to understand ourselves as loveable. As the sustainer of life he also confronts all that is destructive in us, enabling us to celebrate rather than vegetate, and as a friend he hurts when he sees our tendencies to bash ourselves up and others in the process. He cannot resist this alone. He needs our partnership in the exercise. He creates, calls and confronts out of faithfulness to us, in every life and in every moment. The growth that is nurtured when God is responded to is often painful and requires patience, but it is this divine nurture that encourages us to spread our wings and fly in fresher air.

It is the Christian calling to become what we celebrate. If the dynamics of God are to care for what he creates, and heal and enlarge human existence by reconciliation and friendship, then our words are to become flesh even as we speak them. Christian words are uttered for two reasons: first, to adore the mystery and love of God and, second, to be embodied into lives. Service of neighbour, in the spirit of Jesus Christ, is a service to befriend and connect. Serving one another is not as bland as the image of those angelic nurses in sentimental Victorian novels would suggest. It is much more elemental and potent. Christian service connects people, connects hearts with minds, speech with living. It extends the world so that new discoveries can be made. We each have the ability to transfigure situations, in the name of our baptism, so that heaven is brought into the heartland of the ordinary.

So much of life today shrinks humanity rather than awakens it:

> Ego-love doesn't bloom unless it is sheltered. The rules are simple: don't commit yourself to anyone and, therefore, don't allow anyone to come close to you. Simple –

and fateful. Its efforts to shelter its love create a ring of cold around the Ego which slowly eats its way inwards towards the core.[4]

In correction to this trapped situation, the Christian response to finding oneself alive is to work for, and alongside, each other wherever possible as children of the same creator and friend. It also demands resistance when the welfare of brothers and sisters is threatened. Christian belief challenges all selfish talk about the self. But it is when we speak like this as Christians that we are at our most vulnerable.

As the years go by I am becoming more and more sympathetic with the remark of Sir John Quinton that politicians 'are people who, when they see light at the end of the tunnel, order more tunnel'. Of background radio rhetoric, it seems, there is no end. This is nothing new, of course. It was Nye Bevan who commented of Harold Macmillan: 'The Prime Minister has an absolute genius for putting flamboyant labels on empty luggage.'

Mere rhetoric, soothing and persuasive talk that doesn't amount to much at the end of the day, is the enemy within the Church's camp as well as the political one. So often people will say that they would believe in Christ if it wasn't for Christians. Whilst feeling that such sweeping comments distort the truth terribly, I can also find within my own discipleship something quite threatening in such a comment. For whilst I foster a love of Christian living, reflection and speaking, I am also well aware that this love can be sterile. At an extreme level, I am capable of being moved into the heavens (or so I feel) during a liturgy or when reading something about God, but afterwards I am capable of being as shallow, bitter and ungracious as ever I can be. Feeling as I do so often that I am a sort of backbench Christian, I am never more precarious than when saying that as Christians we should be loving.

Recently there has been some interest in Albert Speer,

Hitler's architect and Minister for Armaments.[5] There is debate as to how much he knew about the massacre of the Jews during Hitler's reign. Speer always maintained that he did not know the realities of the situation but opponents claim that he was either lying or in a psychological state in which he convinced himself that he didn't know. Speer's biographer, Gitta Sereny, calls his life a 'battle with truth'.

I know that I am guilty of ignoring truths, the complexities of being called to serve, care for and put myself alongside those placed in my life. When I do it is for my own comfort, but I don't realise it. I can be so far gone down the trail of speaking Christianity that I believe somehow I am living it adequately too. This may not be so and, in fact, Jesus always seemed to be at his most outspoken with those caught up in congratulating themselves on their religious orthodoxy and yet not able to make their belief visible anywhere but in a curtained subculture of jargon, dress and codes. Sometimes we need to be shocked out of our complacency, for it is too easy to live in a twilight world between Christian culture and life unchanged. If Speer did convince himself that he didn't know of human horrors, I am capable, too, of limiting my self-awareness in the name of ideology or a quiet time. However, a thousand genuflections will never hide the truth of how I lived my life.

All authentic life, as understood by Christian faith, is meeting. It is through others that we are inspirited and that a check is kept on our individual prejudices and fantasies. Many argue today that genuine life is competitive, even aggressive, and that 'survival of the fittest' is humanity's natural path – but fit for what? To pursue this form of existence leads to the bizarre situation in which we objectify persons and personalise objects. One sometimes wonders when you watch the advertisements at the cinema or on television today whether the man is having an affair with the woman or the car.

Christian faith is a protest against such a state of affairs that sees the world as a war of egos in what Les Murray has called a

'Kingdom of Flaunt, that unchallenged aristocracy'.[6] Egos define themselves by setting themselves apart from other egos but persons, as intended by God, are created by entering into a closer communion with other persons. Jesus Christ entrusted his future in the world to his friends. They gather to share bread and wine in remembrance of him, and receive life in their communion with him and each other. As the bread and cup are distributed, each receives the same share, and this is the way Christians believe it should be in the world and daily life. All communion is holy and radical. It speaks of human dignity and value as intended by the Creator and communion is fought for and cannot just be expected. It requires a spirit of service, a spirit that is endangered today by so much isolated living, and it calls for patience and much courage. As the poet Mary Oliver reflects:

When it's over, I want to say: all my life
I was a bride married to amazement.
I was the bridegroom, taking the world into my arms.

When it's over, I don't want to wonder
if I made of my life something particular, and real.
I don't want to find myself sighing and frightened,
or full of argument.

I don't want to end up simply having visited this world.[7]

A story is told of a Christian monk who dreamed of going on pilgrimage to Jerusalem. He prayed about it and studied maps and ancient texts for many years until, at last, the abbot gave his permission for the monk to leave the monastery for a year. He was free to walk to the Holy Land and there pray at the sacred sites and walk around the hallowed walls. The day of his release arrived and he set off down the hill from the monastery with staff in hand and his bag on his back.

He had not travelled far before he met a man sitting by the road who told the monk that he and his family were starving and that he was almost too weak now to continue begging for those he loved most. The monk knelt down with the man and prayed and then startled him by walking around him three times before emptying his purse and giving the man his cloak. The monk then turned round and headed back for his monastery where the brothers were amazed to see him. Why had he come back? Had he forgotten something? 'Yes,' replied the monk, 'but now I have been to the Holy Land. Jerusalem was brought to me.' And the tellers of this story concluded by informing their listeners that Christ later appeared to the monk in a vision and revealed that it had been he, the Lord, next to the road that day and that he reminded the monk of the writings of the beloved disciple who taught that the one who says he loves God should love his brother and sister also. Even the monk's piety needed to be humbled in order for his love to be enlarged. Only then was Jerusalem visited.

The glory of God is seen in a person fully alive, a person concerned to befriend and enter into communion wherever possible. Those who want to laugh at us will find it very easy to discover our weaknesses in our trying to become what we celebrate and, likewise, we will know our own failures only too well. Salvation has its torments. Christ's invitation, though, is clear: everything is waiting to be hallowed by the fullness of our being. 'There is another world,' writes Paul Eluard, 'but it is in this one.'

For this reason, when the guests at Babette's feast have made their way home and the two sisters collect their thoughts as to the strange but loving things that have happened that evening, one looks at the dark sky and then into her sister's eyes. 'The stars have come nearer,' she whispers.

seven
LAUGHING

You grow up on the day you have your first real laugh at yourself.

Ethel Barrymore

He deserves Paradise who makes his companions laugh.

The Koran

Time spent laughing is time spent with the gods.

Japanese proverb

I regard it as one of the privileges of my life that, for the last eighteen months of his life, I befriended the actor and comedian Kenneth Williams. He was a legend in his own lifetime, a man with the unique gifts of comic talent, skilled in facial contortion and armed with rich fruity vowels. To watch him perform in front of an audience was to see a man in total control, able to lift those before him and send them into hysterical convulsions at a moment's notice by any anxious director. It is now widely known, due to the publication of his diaries and letters, that Kenneth was a solitary, lonely and, quite often, barbed person. He was capable of middle-distance relating but was unable to bring himself close to another. Like many actors (and, incidentally, many clergy), he was desperate to be looked at but terrified of being seen. My regret is that when he once told me, whilst walking down Great Portland Street, that he had had enough and was 'going to do a Hancock' (that is, commit suicide), I never dreamed that he meant it and simply smiled. It was not long afterwards that I switched on the television news and learned that his body had been discovered in his flat.

Kenneth's natural comedy and pursuit of the outrageous were inseparable from his lonely melancholy. On stage it was as if all that the recluse in him had stored up was sent flying upwards and outwards. Because we could recognise our own aloneness in much of him, and because we could also fall about at his camp, vain and saucy humour, he was a man for all seasons and still commands the interest of the British public.

Like all his fans, I like to remember Kenneth at his funniest. I have burst into a smile as I picture him as Caesar in *Carry On Cleo*, returning from his expeditions abroad to his bored wife Calpurnia, played by the bountiful Joan Sims. She complains that all he does all day is 'conquer, conquer, conquer' and he tries to calm her down by giving her the presents he has brought her. 'Look, dear,' he says, 'I have brought you onions from Spain.'

'I've got Spanish onions!' she snaps.

'And I've brought you cheeses from Holland.'

'I've got Dutch cheeses!' she shouts.

'And here,' the wimpish Caesar proclaims, 'I've brought you precious stones from Gaul.'

'I've got Gaul stones an' all!!' Calpurnia screams at him.

We later see Caesar running away from the fateful dagger of death with the now classic line, 'Infamy! Infamy! They've all got it in for me!'

Laughter is a very large piece of my collage of faith. I can think of no better way of spending time than laughing with family or friends, of sharing jokes and incongruities, and of watching comic genius at work on the stage or screen. Like the narrator of Meera Syal's *Anita and Me*: 'I've always been a sucker for a good double entendre; the gap between what is said and what is thought, what is stated and what is implied, is a place in which I have always found myself.'[1]

To write this book and not mention laughter would be as negligent as failing to mention God. Nothing is as humourless, however, as writing and reading about humour – how it works and why – for the act of bringing it to the surface alters and even destroys the life it has. Like the fish that is caught and pulled onto the shore, explained humour gasps for breath and slowly dies. One needs to let humour be.

Only too conscious of this, I move tentatively on to try and explain why laughter is not only a healthy, fun and sought-after part of my life, but why I believe it is also a necessary ingredient of a life in pursuit of God.

I am aware that much of my life is a rather desperate bid against time and that, in my ambitious attempts to conquer the passing days by finding some sure footing, I get myself into some strange places.

> You have to try. You see a shrink.
> You learn a lot. You read. You think.
> You struggle to improve your looks.
> You meet some men. You write some books.
> You eat good food. You give up junk.
> You do not smoke. You don't get drunk.
> You take up yoga, walk and swim.
> And nothing works. The outlook's grim.
> You don't know what to do. You cry.
> You're running out of things to try.

You blow your nose. You see the shrink.
You walk. You give up food and drink.
You fall in love. You make a plan.
You struggle to improve your man.
And nothing works. The outlook's grim.
You go to yoga, cry, and swim.
You eat and drink. You give up looks.
You struggle to improve your books.
You cannot see the point. You sigh.
You do not smoke. You have to try.[2]

Here as elsewhere Wendy Cope beautifully captures the almosts and the absences that are more than capable of directing our lives. She is equally at home in drawing out the beauty of an ordinary moment and the surprises which keep us moving. Cope's poetry, whether resigned, bleak or touching, holds within it the experiences of contemporary living and feeling and, as such, has revealed parts of me to myself. I have always admired the fact that Cope is not seduced by the ideal but always works hard to maintain honesty. Man, said William Hazlitt, is the only animal that laughs and weeps; for he is the only animal that is stuck with the difference between what things are and what they might have been.

We are people who easily idealise – love ourselves, our memories, our beliefs and abstract notions. It is easy to have, for instance, an ideal picture of what it is to be in love only to discover that your own experiences are not measuring up to it. Ideals can quickly become the enemy of what is good and sufficient to the day. Instead of seeing the integrity, honesty and commonplace goodness of a situation, person, place or viewpoint, we feel they 'fall short' and, with the restlessness of the dissatisfied, begin to look for better.

Ideal notions of what it means to have Christian faith can be particularly damaging. I remember that, when I was ordained and put on my clerical collar for the first time, I walked and talked as if I were an extra from a *Miss Marple* film. My hands would fold themselves piously in front of me when bumping into a parishioner and, at tea, I was almost saying, 'Can I push you to a little more jelly or a sponge finger?' All ridiculous behaviour and an uneasy insecure imitation of artificial role models. It was not long before I realised that little had changed inside me and that I was left, rather disappointingly, with the person who had offered himself for ordination in the first place.

I remember too that, at the time, I thought that I ought to keep a check on my humour when in the parish. After all, it wouldn't be seemly for a priest to be seen laughing loudly in public. Now I just wish they were! It has been said that too many clergy take as their motto in life: 'Start each day with a smile – get it over with.' When I attended a meeting where a foreign bishop, widely known for his seriousness, was delivering an interminable lecture, I thought at one point I saw him smile. I turned to my neighbour: was I right in thinking the bishop had just smiled? 'Don't be silly,' he replied, 'it must have been wind.'

Such grim and grey ecclesiastical elephants are not what we need to further the Kingdom of Heaven. For whether such elephants fight or make love it doesn't matter. It is equally as bad for the lawn. Instead, we need to encourage those like the former Canon at St Paul's cathedral, Sydney Smith, who was confident that 'when wit is combined with sense and information, when it is softened by benevolence and restrained by principle, when it is in the hands of one who loves humour, justice, decency, good nature, morality and religion, wit is then a beautiful part of our nature.'[3]

The comic intrudes into our ordinary daily lives. The interior convulsion that produces a distortion of our features and is accompanied by inarticulate noises, laughter, is infectious and, though intermittent, incurable. It is brought about by the experience of incongruence, and it is because of a similar dislocation – of the other world that permeates and

collides within this one making us 'fools for the sake of Christ'[4]
– that humour has played an essential companion to faith
through the generations. Otherness breaks into the reality we
know.

It is not just within the Christian tradition that the concept
of the 'holy fool' has found a place. There are important
elements of religiously privileged folly in Taoism and Zen
Buddhism, in the primal religions of Africa and the Americas,
and among the wandering *sanyasin* of India. However, the rich
tradition of humour and folly within our Christian heritage has
been very much shadowed by the puritanical spirit. This is a
great loss. We really are fools if we think that by being
humourless we are somehow being more serious and faithful.
The one who laughs has captured an insight and is declaring
a truth. When I laugh at my grandmother, whom I love very
much, I do it out of a deep and trustful relationship and in the
knowledge that our giggles at each other are rituals of affection.
To laugh with God, even at God, religion and faith, can be an
important part of such a trusting dependence.

St Francis described his order of brethren as *ioculatores
Domini,* jokers and jesters of God. It was the Church in the
East, though, that produced the richest collection of such folk.
Theophilus and Maria, who roamed Antioch as a jester and
prostitute, outraging people with bizarre and often obscene
behaviour so that their senses might be changed; St Symeon
who threw walnuts at people in church and ate sausages on
Good Friday; St Basil the Blessed who walked naked through
Moscow and pelted respectable homes with stones; the holy
fools of Novgorod and St Andrew the Fool: all these symbol-
ised in their holy vagabondage the rejection of worldly security
by being perpetual strangers – and perpetually strange. Their
folly is magic as it conjures up another world, a world which
we momentarily glimpse, and reveals that its priorities are
contrary to those of the world it exposes in the same gestures.
The familiar is seen in a new light and becomes strangely

unfamiliar. Eugene Ionesco termed such a transformation in the theatre *depaysement*, literally, losing one's own country. Similarly, Bertolt Brecht described his technique as *Verfremdung*, making strange. The possibilities of the sacred are unearthed. Humour, wrote Kierkegaard, is also the joy which has overcome the world[5] or, in the words of another author:

> To those who do not repudiate the religious insight of the race, the human spirit is uneasy in this world because it is at home elsewhere, and escape from the prison house is possible not only in fancy but in fact. The theist believes in possible beatitude, because he disbelieves in the dignified isolation of humanity. To him, therefore, romantic comedy is serious literature because it is a foretaste of the truth: the Fool is wiser than the Humanist, and clownage is less frivolous than the deification of humanity.[6]

Nietzsche once said that he would find Christianity more convincing if Christians looked more redeemed. It is true that apart from the tradition of the holy fool, humour has not been at the forefront of Christianity's agenda through the ages. When God laughs in the Bible it is usually at people rather than with them, a form of *diasyrm* which basically means 'tearing a person apart'. God always has the last laugh in the Scriptures. On the other hand, St John Chrysostom taught that Jesus never laughed and this dour view took root:

> The negative attitude towards laughter continues in the patristic and medieval periods of Christian thought. There is a long line of grim theologians. Repeatedly there are negative comments on laughter, which is understood as expressing worldliness, sinful insouciance, and lack of faith. Conversely, weeping over the wretchedness of this world is praised as a Christian virtue. Christian saints rarely laugh – except, it seems, in defiance of imminent

martyrdom. Monastic rules proscribed laughter. One does not have to be a Nietschean to loom upon the history of Christian theology as a depressingly lachrymose affair.[7]

As is usual, Christian behaviour may have been rather different from theory at times. Medieval Europe knew a rich comic culture and the unusual liturgical practice of *risus paschalis* was part of it. During the Easter mass the congregation in church was encouraged by the preacher to celebrate the joy of the resurrection with prolonged laughter. If this was difficult to get under way, he would tell amusing stories and jokes – often with obscene elements. It is easy to see why resurrection and laughter were placed together. The limitations of the human condition are overcome by a signal of transcendence. Life is made alive, given energies and taught to recognise the absurdities of an adventure-less existence. If laughter confronts the daily incongruities of life, faith confronts the ultimate ones.

The Shakespearean fools are usually multi-layered characters. The fool in *King Lear*, for instance, is loyal, truth telling and able to level a situation by his songs and wisdom. He has always seemed to be a good role model for a bishop's chaplain. The wit and humour of a fool is able to find reserves of loyalty towards those he serves. He dares to speak the truth to those who don't want to hear and, when life is being torn apart by extremes, heat of passion or fickle moods, he is a calming influence, placing things in proper proportion. A Christian life has a similar vocation and is more likely to succeed with the help of laughter.

It is also interesting to note that the Holy Spirit has traditionally been understood as having the qualities that we can also see in kind, not hurtful, humour. The Holy Spirit is both Comforter and Disturber, and humour, too, acts as both of these as it shocks you into recognition and a sense of renewed place. The levelling that humour can bring about is essential to those of us who can so easily be tempted into vanity. It is said that you can always tell which denomination's vestry you are in by looking around you. In a Methodist vestry you will always see a large picture of the Good Shepherd hanging on the wall. In a Roman Catholic vestry you will always see a large crucifix in prime place. You know when you are in an Anglican vestry, though, by the full-length mirror . . . We need to watch ourselves; we can easily glide into grand notions of our importance and talents, and become obsessed with appearances or presentation. Laughter, at its best, places its companions on an equal footing and, like the Holy Spirit again, has an inclusive nature, seeking out ways of bringing in rather than forcing exclusion.

Likewise, the temptations and bubbles of ambition can be pricked by the rug being pulled out from under our feet. Ambition is no stranger to the Christian community. There is a telling story of a holy monk in the desert who spent his days in prayer and fasting, weeping for his sins and the sins of the world. The demons were very keen to bring him down and tempted him with everything that had worked on people in the past: drink, sex, food and money. Nothing would tempt the monk away from his holy cell, however, and the demons went to rest under a tree because they were worn out and needed to think of a new strategy.

As they were resting, the Devil himself came up to them and asked them what the matter was. They explained the situation and how all their best temptations had failed. The Devil told them to wait there. He went over to the monk, bent down and whispered into his ear. All of a sudden the monk screamed with horror, blasphemed, pulled his cross off his neck and threw all his sacred books out of the cell. The demons were amazed and were keen to ask the Devil what it was he had said to the holy man. 'It was quite simple,' he replied, 'I told him his brother had just been elected the Bishop of Antioch.'

Ambitions can draw you away from yourself into a calculating, often charming, disrespectful player of games that can damage human relationships. We only need think of so-called 'Nasty Nick' in the *Big Brother* television programme for an example of what we are all capable of in varying degrees each and every day. The Danes have a typically robust proverb to warn us: 'The more the monkey climbs up the tree, the more you see of its bottom.' Beware!

As well as a poetic Church, then, I would hope that we might dare to be a laughing Church. We are often on the verge of being too serious and introverted, so much so that when we do attempt a joke or two we look artificial and limp. It would be much healthier if we could use humour as an essential theological tool in the serious enterprise of salvation. As Peter L. Berger has argued, what the Catholic theologian Hugo Rahner writes about the significance of play might also be applied to a new significance of the comic within the Church:

> To play is to yield oneself to a kind of magic, to enact to oneself the absolutely other, to pre-empt the future, to give the lie to the inconvenient world of fact. In play earthly realities become, of a sudden, things of the transient moment, presently left behind, then disposed of and buried in the past; the mind is prepared to accept the unimagined and incredible, to enter a world where different laws apply, to be relieved of all the weights that bear it down, to be free, kingly, unfettered and divine. Man at play is reaching out . . . for that superlative ease, in which even the body, freed from its earthly burden, moves to the effortless measures of a heavenly dance.[8]

For all the reasons I have cited, then, I also think there is a place for irony in Christian life and words. Irony is notoriously difficult to define. Plato regarded it as 'dissimulation' and the *eiron* referred to by Theophrastus was the one who was 'slippery in his speech'. In 1502 an English definition emerged which is more helpful. It is that 'by whiche a man sayeth one &

gyveth to understande the contrarye'. It later became known as 'drie mock', a form of gentle but purposeful mockery. By the middle of the eighteenth century a whole host of authors from Swift to Fielding, Dryden to Pope, had displayed a fine literary command of irony and it has continued to thrive in England ever since.

Kierkegaard believed that irony was, for the Christian, an 'excellent surgeon' and that 'if one must warn against irony as a seducer, one must also praise it as a guide'. He argued that it was irony that 'actualizes actuality', dispelling illusion, hypocrisy and deceit, and bringing the truth of a situation into clear focus. As D.C. Muecke asserts, we shall not view a situation as ironic unless we believe there are those, somewhere or other, who do not.[9] It has a corrective function. Because religion is never quite as straightforward as it may appear ('to a large extent what people do with their lunacy: their phobias, their will to power, their sexual frustrations'[10]), irony is able to find a home amongst us to pull us down when we raise ourselves too high up. One of the best descriptions of irony I have come across, and one which reveals its necessity, is in Robertson Davies' novel *The Cunning Man*:

> I had become wiser, I tried to find out what irony really is, and discovered some ancient writer on poetry had spoken of 'Ironia, which we call the drye mock', and I cannot think of a better term for it. Not sarcasm, which is like vinegar, or cynicism, which is so often the voice of disappointed idealism, but a delicate casting of a cool and illuminating light on life, and thus an enlargement. The ironist is not bitter, he does not seek to undercut everything that seems worthy or serious, he scorns the cheap scoring-off of the wisecracker. He stands, so to speak, somewhat at one side, observes and speaks with a moderation which is occasionally embellished with a flash of controlled exaggeration. He speaks from certain depth,

and thus he is not of the same nature as the wit, who so often speaks from the tongue and no deeper. The wit's desire is to be funny; the ironist is only funny as a secondary achievement.[11]

I believe that laughter is one of the largest and most essential patches on my collage. To be able to laugh brings change and possibility into your life as you view yourself, your limitations and foibles, your absurdities and enjoyments, in a strong light. It is, for me, a holy act. As Peter L. Berger sums up so well: 'The experience of the comic is, finally, a promise of redemption. Religious faith is the intuition (some lucky people would say the conviction) that the promise will be kept.'[12]

postscript

Synthesis, say the heavens. Analysis, says man.

Victor Hugo

**God was in the spaces, he was sure. God went to the
very edges of the page.**

Jim Crace

The trouble is I don't believe my unbelief.

Graham Greene

At the end of a short book like this, I take comfort in the
advice of Quentin Crisp: 'If at first you don't succeed, failure
may be your style.' It is a book which, as I said in the Prologue,
has no beginning, middle and end for such containment does
not ring true to my experience of living nor to my experience
of Christian faith. It attempts to throw light on the collage of
God that I find myself building but, as such, it is simply a very
small fragment of a much larger confession proclaimed by the
Christian Church. In the spirit of Nennius' introduction to his
Historia Brittonum: 'I have made a heap of all that I could find.'

In a short story by the brilliantly intelligent and imaginative writer Jorge Luis Borges, a man very influenced by Kafka, we find a theologian who, after death, has discovered himself in a new world. Picking up his pen,

> . . . he began to write something about charity; but what he wrote on the paper one day, he did not see the next; for this happens to everyone there when he commits anything to paper from the external man only, and not at the same time from the internal, thus from compulsion and not from freedom; it is obliterated of itself . . .[1]

It is my hope that something of this book will last long enough for those who have been, and are still, the encouragers in my life to understand something of my thoughts and experiences of God as they weave in and out of each other today. As Toni Morrison has argued,[2] when we wake from a dream we always want to remember all of it although the small fragment that we are remembering is probably the most important part. The pieces of the collage I have introduced here are mere scraps of fabric of a much greater creation. They are important fragments that begin to outline a soul's shaping and architecture, a small exposition of a truth of which George Herbert speaks:

> My searches are my daily bread;
> Yet never prove.[3]

They are also the fragments to which I turn when I try to recover my first love, to kindle again the adoration of God that seized my soul as a young boy in Shropshire when I found myself strolling along country lanes and into a tiny church. It was there that I first knelt, and wept, at the beauty of something I didn't comprehend.

In his preface to the play *Miss Julie* the Swedish dramatist August Strindberg describes how he creates his characters:

> I have drawn my people as split and vacillating, a mixture

> of the old and the new . . . My souls are agglomerations
> of past and present cultures, scraps from books and news-
> papers, fragments of humanity, torn shreds of once-fine
> clothing that has become rags, in just the way that a
> human soul is patched together.[4]

I know my soul to be made of such patches. I am not able to
explain them; all I can try and do is capture some of them on
paper and then cross-reference with others. Somebody once
noted that a true pastor is concerned about his or her own soul
and others' bodies, not his or her body and others' souls. I have
not reached such maturity, but I am trying more and more to
understand the chemistry of my own spirit in order that I might
also be freed to discover more and more friends to meet and
converse with.

As a person living in the United Kingdom in the twenty-first
century, I am more than aware of my ability to be chameleon-
like and, encouraged by much of our culture, turn various
shades of grey. We struggle for footing in a world that pulls us
this way and that every minute of the day. At our best, we
watch ourselves closely to resist being carried away by popular
opinion. Obedience to the law of gravity, as Simone Weil
knew, can be the greatest sin.[5] Geoffrey Hill's characteristically
sharp exposure of our times rings true in my weaker parts:

> Take out supposition. Insert suppository.
> For definitely the right era, read: deaf in the right ear.[6]

It is my thorough conviction, at the same time, that Christian
faith brings with it a necessary colour and depth, releasing
existence into life. It is also my conviction that there is a whole
world of unexplored words, images and ambiguities revolving
around belief in God that might yet resonate and build the
kingdom in our empty spaces.

As the parish priest of St Paul's, Covent Garden, I am in

constant touch with members of the theatre community. St Paul's is affectionately called 'the Actors' Church'. The present ongoing debate about the future of the theatre has many similarities with the Church's discussions about its own future. Is success marked by the number of tickets sold? How can smaller theatre productions compete with blockbuster musicals with their vast sources of funding? Is there still value in live theatre when the vast entertainment industry is so developed and universal? What does it have to say to our times anyway?

I have found Benedict Nightingale's answers to some of these questions regarding the future of the theatre comparable to my own conclusions regarding that of the Christian Church. Nightingale argues for a theatre where profound, elusive and unique senses are generated and shared. He believes that a major task of future directors will be to join the playwrights of tomorrow in teaching us to listen, speak and think less thinly. He concludes that 'The theatre may be the last place where we can gather together and, helped by a few actors, construct dreams and share fancies. It will be a gymnasium for underused imaginations'.[7]

Peter Brook has also been arguing for many years now that the invisible currents that rule our lives need to be caught by the theatre's art, for 'we know that the world of appearances is a crust – under the crust is the boiling matter we see if we peer into a volcano . . . To comprehend the visibility of the invisible is a life's work'.[8]

It appears to me that both the Church and the theatre are focused on the horizon, on what can be seen when we look up out of ourselves and seek the wider view. To this end, the vocations of the Church and Theatre are inseparably linked. Both are committed to heightened perception. Whereas much of the theatre's view of the horizon is horizontal, keeping level with human beings because it is their world, the Church wants to shake the horizon and tilt it so that it edges towards being vertical. It then transforms into a channel between the sacred and the human, the 'trembling roadway' that the Norse myths embodied in the rainbow. Where the vertical horizon is glimpsed, the rumour of God is alive and the Church becomes a place for 'underused imaginations' too. It will be keeping alive rumours of a God who is 'Invisible, unprovable, perhaps, and shy to intervene. But ready to provide'.[9] I believe these rumours to be true.

I have tried to argue that it is a confidently, poetic, truthful, laughing, serving, prayerful Church that will be able to share conversations with such a world about a hidden God who reveals to us all we need to discover. On Robert Frost's white marble grave it reads: 'I had a lover's quarrel with the world.' It may well be that the Church will have such a quarrel too, but if it ever stops talking with the world because it feels it has a truth within that is easily contaminated we will have simply decided to lay down our calling to be salt in the earth and yeast in the bread. Then, we might as well be like the Clangers in the children's television programme, living in our own world with our own untranslatable language and just occasionally daring to send off a rocket to see if it might ever be possible to communicate with someone else. This Clanger religion is not, in the words of Proverbs, 'good news from a far country'[10] because it can't be heard or translated by those who encounter it. It was Quentin Crisp, again, who summed up Liberace by commenting, 'as he grew more artificial he became more genuine'. God forbid that the Church and its theology should go the same way in the search for a renewed identity.

When Moses asked the Holy One his name, he replied, '*Eh'yeh asher eh'yeh*' – 'I shall be who I shall be'.[11] In other words, God does not define himself in the present, his very name is a projection into the future. This, for me at least, is our sacred hope, a hope that 'is not the conviction that something will turn out well but that something makes sense regardless'.[12] It is a hope that won't ever quite let me go, a hope that prompts me to place the next piece on the collage which is a poem by R.S. Thomas who once said in a letter that he has been trying 'to operate on as many levels as possible, mostly failing, being self-contradictory, open to refutation on the charge of inconsistency, but occasionally perhaps setting up overtones'.[13]

In this desert of language
    we find ourselves in,
with the sign-post with the word 'God'
    worn away

           and the distance?
Pity the simpleton
    with his mouth open crying:
           How far is it to God?
And the wiseacre says: Where you were,
friend.
    You know that smile
           glossy
as the machine that thinks it has outpaced
    belief?
           I am one of those
who sees from the arms opened
           to embrace the future
the shadow of the Cross fall
    on the smoothest of surfaces
           causing me to stumble.[14]

notes

Prologue

1. These friends know who they are and, I hope, realise how grateful I shall always be to them. I will not embarrass them by naming them here, but they are loved and remembered very much.
2. Isaiah Berlin, 'The Hedgehog and the Fox: An Essay on Tolstoy's View of History' in *The Proper Study of Mankind: An Anthology of Essays* (Pimlico, 1998), p. 436.
3. ibid., p. 436.
4. ibid., p. 491.
5. Kate Atkinson, *Behind the Scenes at the Museum* (Black Swan, 1997), p. 382.
6. Virginia Woolf, *To the Lighthouse* (Granada, 1985), p. 172.
7. Iris Murdoch, *The Sovereignty of Good* (Routledge and Kegan Paul, 1970), p. 95.
8. Isak Dinesen, 'The Cardinal's First Tale' in *Last Tales* (Penguin, 1986), p. 26.

Chapter 1: Hiddenness

1. Dennis Potter, *Seeing the Blossom: Two Interviews and a Lecture* (Faber and Faber, 1994), pp. 5–6.
2. Richard Wilbur, 'For Dudley' in *Walking to Sleep* (Faber, 1971), p. 25.
3. Edwin Muir, 'The Way' in *The Complete Poems* (Association for Scottish Literary Studies, 1991), p. 159.
4. Quoted in John Pick, *Gerard Manley Hopkins: Priest and Poet* (Oxford University Press, 1966), p. 129.
5. Mary Bryden, 'Saints and Stereotypes: The Case of Thérèse of Lisieux' in *Literature and Theology*, Vol. 13, No. 1, March 1999, p. 14.
6. A.S. Byatt, 'Christ in the House of Martha and Mary' in *Elementals* (Chatto and Windus, 1998), p. 226.
7. Ian McEwan, *Enduring Love* (Jonathan Cape, 1997), p. 30.
8. William Shakespeare, *King Lear*, Act V, scene 3.

NOTES

9. D.Z. Phillips, *From Fantasy to Faith* (Macmillan, 1991), p. 207.
10. Luke 24:51.
11. John 9:41.
12. Clement of Alexandria, *Miscellanies*, V, 11.
13. Roland Barthes, quoted in Rubem A. Alves, *The Poet, The Warrior, The Prophet* (SCM, 1990,), p. 1.
14. Exodus 20:21, 24.
15. Genesis 32:22–31.
16. For example Psalms 22 and 35.
17. Gregory of Nyssa, *The Life of Moses*, tr. Abraham J. Malherbe and Everett Ferguson (Paulist Press, 1978), p. 94.
18. Rubem A. Alves' work is always highly rewarding to read. Chapter 1 of *The Poet, The Warrior, The Prophet* argues for the importance of 'unlearning' – in the spirit of Meister Eckhart, perhaps, who wrote that 'only the hand that erases can write the true thing'. Alves also relates that the philosopher Lessing once said that if God offered him, in his right hand, the knowledge of the whole truth, and in his left, the perennial search for truth, with all the dangers and disappointments that this entails, he would opt for the left hand . . .
19. R.S. Thomas, 'The Empty Church' in *Collected Poems 1945–1990* (J.M. Dent, 1993), p.349.
20. R. S. Thomas, 'Abercuawg' in *Selected Prose* (Poetry Wales Press, 1983), p. 153.
21. ibid., p. 17.
22. R.S. Thomas, 'Somewhere' in *Collected Poems*.
23. Henry Vaughan, 'The Night' in *The Metaphysical Poets*, ed. Helen Gardner (Penguin, 1983), p. 281.
24. W.B. Yeats, 'Crazy Jane Talks With the Bishop', in *Collected Poems* (Papermac, 1982), p. 295.
25. In *The Oxford Book of Prayer*, ed. George Appleton (Oxford University Press, 1988), p. 119.
26. David Jones, *The Anathemata* (Faber and Faber, 1972, first published 1952).
27. Anne Michaels, *Fugitive Pieces* (Bloomsbury, 1997), p. 107.

Chapter 2: Discovery

1. Jane Hamilton, *A Map of the World* (Black Swan, 1996).
2. Philip Toynbee, *Part of a Journey* (Collins, 1981), 15 February 1978 entry.
3. John Searle, *Mind, Language and Society: Philosophy in the Real World* (Weidenfeld and Nicolson, 1999), p. 79.
4. John Donne, Sermon preached at St Paul's upon Christmas Day, 1624, in *Selected Prose* (Penguin, 1987), p. 221.

5. T.S. Eliot, 'The Dry Salvages, II', in *Collected Poems* (Faber and Faber, 1989), p. 208.

6. R.S. Thomas, from 'Adjustments' in *Collected Poems 1945–1990* (J.M. Dent, 1993), p. 345.

7. John Dominic Crossan, 'Waking the Bible' in *Interpretation* 32 (1978), pp. 265–85.

8. Elie Wiesel, *All Rivers Run to the Sea: Memoirs Volume One 1928–1969* (HarperCollins, 1997), p. 49.

9. Dietrich Bonhoeffer, *Meditating on the Word* (Eng. Cambridge, Mass: Cowley Publictions, 1986), p. 45.

10. U.A. Fanthorpe, from 'Getting It Across' in *Selected Poems* (Penguin, 1986), p. 73.

11. R.S. Thomas, from 'The Kingdom' in *Collected Poems 1945–1990*, p. 233.

12. A.M. Ramsey, *God, Christ and the World* (SCM, 1969), p. 98.

13. Ted Hughes, from *Crow* (Faber and Faber, 1974).

14. John V. Taylor, *The Christlike God* (SCM, 1992), p. 205.

15. ibid., p. 205.

16. John Chrysostom, *Paschal Homily* (Office of Matins for Easter in the Byzantine Rite).

17. Dag Hammarskjold, *Markings* (Faber and Faber, 1964), p. 77.

18. ibid., p. 52.

19. Peter Hoeg, *Miss Smilla's Feeling for Snow* (Flamingo, 1994), p. 142.

20. Bruno Bettelheim, *The Informed Heart* (Penguin, 1991), preface.

21. Nicolas Cabasilas, quoted in Olivier Clement, *On Human Being: A Spiritual Anthropology* (New City, 2000), p. 21.

22. Anna Akhmatova, *Sochineniia*, Vol. 2 (Moscow, 1986), p. 205.

23. Quoted in Michael Mayne, *Pray, Love, Remember* (DLT, 1998), p. 45.

Chapter 3: Poetry

1. Dag Hammarskjold, *Markings* (Faber and Faber, 1964), p. 101.

2. Northrop Frye, *The Great Code* (London, 1983), p. 60.

3. Neil Carrick, 'Daniil Kharms: Theologian of the Absurd', *Birmingham Slavonic Monographs*, No. 28, 1988, p. 9.

4. M. Arnold, 'The Study of Poetry' in *Essays in Criticism: Second Series* (London: Macmillan, 1888), p. 663.

5. Anne Stevenson, 'The Minister' in *The Collected Poems 1955–1995* (Oxford University Press, 1996), p. 62.

6. Quoted in Kenneth Leech, *True Prayer: An Introduction to Christian Spirituality* (Sheldon Press, 1980), p. 10.

7. Paul Avis, 'God and the Creative Imagination: Metaphor, Symbol and Myth' in *Religion and Theology* (Routledge, 1999), p. 7.

8. For a more detailed discussion of these matters, see my, 'God – to be or

NOTES

not to be', Farmington Papers No. MT2, The Farmington Institute for Christian Studies, 1994.

9. *Notes for Newcomers* for Sea of Faith III Conference, 1990.

10. William Shakespeare, *The Tempest,* Epilogue spoken by Prospero.

11. Maurice Wiles's review in *Theology,* XCVII, No. 776, March/April, 1994, p. 130, of Anthony Freeman's *God in Us* (SCM, 1993).

12. Brian Russell, 'With Respect to Don Cupitt' in *Theology,* LXXXVIII, No. 721, January 1985, p. 5.

13. RowanWilliams, 'Religious Realism' in *Modern Theology,* 4, 1984.

14. Seamus Heaney, 'Lightenings' in *Seeing Things* (Faber and Faber, 1991), p. 62.

15. Seamus Heaney, *The Redress of Poetry: Oxford Lectures* (Faber and Faber, 1995), p. xiii.

16. George Herbert, 'Prayer' in *The Metaphysical Poets,* ed. Helen Gardner (Penguin, 1983), p. 124.

17. Heaney, *The Redress of Poetry,* p. 8.

18. J.H. Newman, *Essays Critical and Historical,* Vol. 1 (London and New York, 1895), p. 23.

19. See Virginia Woolf's *To the Lighthouse* (Granada, 1985), p. 150.

20. R.S. Thomas, from 'After Jericho' in *Collected Poems 1945–1990* (J.M. Dent, 1993), p. 356.

21. Gustave Flaubert, *Madame Bovary* (Oxford University Press, 1991), p. xix.

22. A.C. Thisleton, *Language, Liturgy and Meaning* (Grove Books, 1975).

23. H. Schmidt, 'Language and its Function in Christian Worship' in *Studia Liturgica,* 8 (1971–2), p. 8.

24. From 'Words: For Wendell Berry' in K. Raine, *Living With Mystery: Poems 1987–91* (Golgonooza Press, 1992), p. 39.

25. Gail Ramshaw, *Worship Searching for Language* (Pastoral Press, 1988), p. 112.

26. T.S. Eliot, *The Rock,* Chorus III, 7–8 in *Collected Poems 1909–1962* (Faber and Faber, 1989), p. 169.

27. Wislawa Szymborska, 'The Poet and the World: Nobel Lecture 1996' in *Poems New and Collected 1957–1997* (Faber and Faber, 1998), p. xvi.

28. Quoted in Andrew Motion, *Philip Larkin: A Writer's Life* (Faber and Faber, 1993), p. 47.

29. James Cowan, *A Mapmaker's Dream* (Sceptre, 1996), p. 14.

30. From 'Poetry and Religion' in Les Murray, *Collected Poems* (Carcanet, 1991), pp. 272–3.

Chapter 4: Truthfulness

1. Peter Hoeg, *Miss Smilla's Feeling for Snow* (Flamingo, 1994), p. 135.
2. Czeslaw Milosz, *The Captive Mind* (Penguin, 1981), p. xii.
3. Dietrich Bonhoeffer, *Letters and Papers from Prison*, ed. Eberhard Bethge (New York: Macmillan, 1972), p. 310.
4. Carolyn M. Jones, 'Dietrich Bonhoeffer's Letters and Papers from Prison: Rethinking the Relationship of Theology and Arts, Literature and Religion' in *Literature and Theology*, Vol. 9, No. 3, September 1995, p. 244.
5. John Dagenais, *The Ethics of Reading in Manuscript Culture* (Princeton, 1994). See also Joyce Coleman, *Public Reading and the Reading Public in Late Medieval England and France* (New York, 1996).
6. George Steiner, 'The Uncommon Reader' in *No Passion Spent: Essays 1978–1996* (Faber and Faber, 1997), p. 1.
7. R.S. Thomas, 'Raptor' in *No Truce with the Furies* (Bloodaxe, 1995), p. 52.
8. A quip of Mencken quoted in Steiner, *No Passion Spent*, p. 9.
9. Justin Wintle in an article entitled 'A Long Goodbye to Berlin', in the *Independent* on 31 October 1998.
10. Iris Murdoch, *Henry and Cato* (Penguin, 1977), p. 398.
11. Franz Kafka, letter to Oskar Pollak, 27 January 1904: see *Briefe 1902–1924* (S. Fischer Verlag, 1958, pp. 27f.).
12. W.H. Auden, 'Song VIII' in *Collected Poems* (Faber and Faber, 1994), p. 140.
13. Ian McEwan, *Amsterdam* (Jonathan Cape, 1998), p. 71.
14. Eleanor Bron, *Life and other Punctures.*
15. Pascal, *Pensées* (Penguin, 1966), p. 131.
16. Erich Auerbach, *Mimesis: The Representation of Reality in Western Literature* (New York: Garden City, 1957), p. 138.
17. 'The hood does not make the monk': Lucio to Escalus in William Shakespeare, *Measure for Measure*, V, i.
18. Elie Wiesel, *All Rivers Run To The Sea: Memoirs, Volume I 1928–1969* (HarperCollins, 1997), p.16.
19. W.H. Auden, 'Whitsunday in Kirchstetten' in *Collected Poems* (Faber and Faber, 1994), p. 743.
20. Alfred Kerr in 1905, cited in the programme for Trevor Nunn's excellent production of Ibsen's *The Enemy of the People* at the National Theatre in 1997–8.

Chapter 5: Praying

1. Robert Pinsky, *Poetry and the World* (New York: Ecco Press, 1988), p. 85.
2. Ted Hughes, *Tales from Ovid: Twenty-four Passages from the Metamorphoses* (Faber and Faber, 1997), p. 10.

3. Wisława Szymborska, 'Nothing's A Gift' in *Poems New and Collected 1957–1997* (Faber and Faber, 1998), p. 252.

4. George Herbert, from 'Prayer (1)' in *Oxford Poetry Library* (Oxford University Press, 1994), p. 40.

5. St Symeon, cited in Kenneth Leech, *True Prayer: An Introduction to Christian Spirituality* (Sheldon Press, 1980), p. 3.

6. Seamus Heaney, in his Nobel lecture in Stockholm, published as *Crediting Poetry* (The Gallery Press, 1996), p. 20.

7. John Galsworthy, *The Silver Spoon*.

8. Wendy Cope, 'Strugnell's Christian Song 3' in *Serious Concerns* (Faber and Faber, 1992), p. 62.

9. Origen, *On Prayer*, 12, Patrologia Graeca, Migne, 11,452.

10. John V. Taylor, *The Christlike God* (SCM, 1992), p. 261.

11. Tony Harrison, *Plays 1: The Mysteries* (Faber and Faber, 1985).

12. Alan Ecclestone, quoted in David Scott, *Moments of Prayer* (SPCK, 1997), p. 80.

13. Mark Jarman, 'Psalm: First Forgive the Silence' in *Image: A Journal of the Arts and Religion*, Spring 1995, No. 9, p. 26.

14. Soren Kierkegaard, *Christian Discourses*, quoted in Michael Mayne, *This Sunrise of Wonder* (Fount, 1995), p. 288.

15. R.S. Thomas, from 'Kneeling' in *Collected Poems*, p. 199.

16. ibid., p. 517.

Chapter 6: Service

1. Isak Dinesen (Karen Blixen), *Anecdotes of Destiny* (Penguin, 1986), p. 23.

2. John 15:15.

3. Dinah Maria Mulock, in her novel *A Life for a Life* (1859).

4. Dag Hammarskjold, *Markings* (Faber and Faber, 1964), p. 54.

5. See, for instance, Gitta Sereny's biography, *Albert Speer: His Battle with Truth* (Picador, 1976), and David Edgar's play *Albert Speer.* (Nick Hern Books, 2000)

6. Les Murray, 'The Dream of Wearing Shorts Forever' in *Collected Poems* (Carcanet, 1998), p. 235.

7. Mary Oliver, 'When Death Comes' in *New and Selected Poems* (Boston: Beacon Press, 1992), p. 10.

Chapter 7: Laughing

1. Meera Syal, *Anita and Me* (Flamingo, 1997), p. 10.

2. Wendy Cope, 'Some More Light Verse' in *Serious Concerns* (Faber and Faber, 1992), p. 8.

3. Quoted in *The Smith of Smiths* (Carr's Books).

4. 1 Corinthians 4:10.

NOTES

5. Howard Hong and Edna Hong (eds.), *Soren Kierkegaard's Journals and Papers*, Vol. 2 (Bloomington: Indiana University Press), p. 262.

6. Enid Welsford, *The Fool* (Garden City, New York: Anchor, 1956), pp. 326f.

7. Peter L. Berger: *Redeeming Laughter: The Comic Dimension of Human Experience* (Walter de Gruyter, 1997), p. 198.

8. Hugo Rahner, *Man at Play* (Burns and Oates, 1965), pp. 65f.

9. See his *Irony and the Ironic* (Methuen, 1986).

10. H.A. Williams, *Some Day I'll Find You* (Mitchell Beazley, 1982), p. 214.

11. Robertson Davies, *The Cunning Man* (Penguin, 1995), p. 150.

12. Berger, *Redeeming Laughter*, p. x.

Postscript

1. Jorge Luis Borges, 'Et cetera' in *Collected Fictions* (Penguin, 2000), p. 54.

2. Toni Morrison, 'Memory, Creation and Writing' in *Thought* 59:235, December 1984, p. 388.

3. George Herbert, 'The Search' in *Oxford Poetry Library* (Oxford University Press, 1994), p. 142.

4. August Strindberg, 'Preface to *Miss Julie*' in *The Plays*, Vol. 1, tr. Michael Meyer (Secker and Warburg, 1964), p. 103.

5. See, for instance, Simone Petrement, *Simone Weil* (Pantheon, 1976), or Weil's own *La Pesanteur et la Grace*.

6. *Geoffrey Hill, The Triumph of Love: A Poem* CV (Penguin, 1999), p. 54.

7. Benedict Nightingale, *The Future of Theatre* (Phoenix, 1998), p. 39.

8. Peter Brook, *The Empty Space* (Penguin, 1990), pp. 58 and 63.

9. Jim Crace, *Quarantine* (Penguin, 1998), p. 108.

10. Proverbs 25:25.

11. Exodus 3:14.

12. Vaclav Havel, *Disturbing the Peace* (Faber and Faber, 1990), p. 181.

13. Quoted in D.Z. Phillip's preface to *R.S. Thomas, Poet of the Hidden God: Meaning and Mediation in the Poetry of R.S. Thomas* (Macmillan, 1986), p. ix.

14. R.S. Thomas, 'Directions', in *Collected Poems 1945–1990* (J.M. Dent, 1993), p. 374.